# WORKS OF BERTOLT BRECHT

*The Grove Press Edition*

*General Editor: Eric Bentley*

*Translators*

Lee Baxandall

Eric Bentley

Martin Esslin

N. Goold-Verschoyle

H. R. Hays

Anselm Hollo

Christopher Isherwood

Frank Jones

Charles Laughton

Carl R. Mueller

Desmond I. Vesey

Richard Winston

## Previously Published

*The Caucasian Chalk Circle*

*Edward II*

*Galileo*

*The Good Woman of Setzuan*

*The Jewish Wife and Other Short Plays*

*Jungle of Cities and Other Plays*

*Manual of Piety*

*The Mother*

*Mother Courage and Her Children*

*Selected Poems of Bertolt Brecht*

*Seven Plays by Bertolt Brecht*

*Threepenny Novel*

*The Threepenny Opera*

*The Visions of Simone Machard*
*(with Lion Feuchtwanger)*

# Baal
# A Man's A Man

*and*

# The Elephant Calf

Early plays by Bertolt Brecht

*Edited and with Introductions by*

ERIC BENTLEY

*An Evergreen Black Cat* 🐱 *Book*

GROVE PRESS, INC.     NEW YORK

Library of Congress Catalog Card Number: 64-13781

Fifth Printing

MANUFACTURED IN THE UNITED STATES OF AMERICA

DISTRIBUTED BY RANDOM HOUSE, INC., NEW YORK

# CONTENTS

# Baal

# INTRODUCTION

## Bertolt Brecht's First Play

The fame of Brecht's later plays has been bad for the reputation of his earlier ones, and in combating this phenomenon one is combating some powerful preconceptions. It is assumed, for example, that a major writer steadily improves. Early works are automatically placed in such categories as juvenilia and apprenticeship. Also, the earlier work is judged by criteria suggested by the later. Brecht himself judged his early work by criteria suggested by the later, which compounded the problem and created the cliché. The cliché reads as follows: "The later Brecht was a great man who had found himself in finding a great philosophy. The early Brecht was a confused and misguided young fellow who would never have come to any good—had he not found the great philosophy and, through it, his greater self. In other words, the early work represents the sin from which Marxism redeemed him. The early Brecht is the unregenerate Saul; the late Brecht, the sainted Paul." Now this cliché is the more important because it is taken over—with a little rewording—by many non-Marxists. It can be taken over without misgivings by anyone who is prepared to assume that to go from despair and pessimism to some sort of "positive" philosophy is to become a finer artist.

To protest at this cliché should not be to reverse it. An artist is not confronted with the alternative: progress or regress. Merely development—with ups and downs—is more normal. And that in my view is what the career of Brecht has to show. This, however, must be said on behalf of his early work: that had he died immediately after

3

writing it, he would in time have been classed with other such youths of amazing poetic genius as Büchner and Rimbaud.

*In time.* His work, like theirs, could not be assimilated by the contemporary public. It was too original. In any case, the broader public only takes up "unpopular" work on the basis of some misunderstanding. Brecht himself was to become popular through misunderstanding when the German bourgeoisie would take *The Threepenny Opera* to its big clammy bosom in the belief that the philosophy of the piece was summed up in "Erst kommt das Fressen, dann kommt die Moral." If an author cannot be understood, it is important—for his bankbook at least—that he be misunderstood. But *Baal* did not get across in either way. It was intelligible, in the nineteen-twenties, only to persons who themselves had unusual insight into our life and times. In a prologue which Hofmannsthal wrote for the Viennese première in 1926,* the poet put his finger on the very pulse of the play. ". . . all the ominous events of Europe," says one of his spokesmen, "which we have witnessed these last twelve years are nothing but a long drawn out way of laying the weary concept of the European individual in the grave . . ." Oscar Homolka, who played Baal, was given this speech by Hofmannsthal: "We are anonymous forces. Psychological possibilities. Individuality is one of the fantastic embellishments which we have stripped from us. You'll see how I'm going to play Baal."

We are taught in school about "the end of heroism" in the drama of the eighteenth and nineteenth centuries. The hero of tragedy was replaced by the individual of the nineteenth-century novel and play. Ibsen's work is par excel-

---

* Hugo von Hofmannsthal wrote a Prologue for the first Viennese performance of the play in 1926. In it the members of the Company played themselves, and so we find parts written for Oscar Homolka, Egon Friedell, Hermann Thimig, and their producer Herbert Waniek. Alfred Schwarz's English version of this Prologue was published in the Brecht Issue of *Tulane Drama Review*, Autumn 1961.

lence the drama of that individual. Yet even here, where the dramatis personae are most individual, individuality is seen as threatened. Failing to be a hero, Master Builder Solness manages to be an individual—but only just, for the threat of complete disintegration is ever-present. In the dream plays of Strindberg the individual is dissolving in mist and mysticism. Instead of personalities there are memories, bits of experience, cross-references, images, names, momentary encounters. In Pirandello's plays of around 1920 the non-existence of the individual is proclaimed. But to sustain the form of a play, Pirandello reverts to the traditional types, a little dressed up in Ibsenish "biography." Hence there is an element of contradiction between the *theory* that there is no such thing as continuity in character, and the presentation, *in practice*, of people who are continuous and of a piece. Yet Pirandello does more than state the idea of discontinuity: he also projects the state of soul of those who believe in this idea, those who feel discontinuous with themselves, the disoriented, the metaphysically as well as neurotically lost: men of the twentieth century.

*Baal* is neither a Strindbergian dream play, nor a Pirandellian "play in the making." What was in part a theory for the older men is here wholly a practice, a state of being, a fact of life. Few of us did see how Homolka played Baal, yet the script itself suggests vividly enough the truth of his remarks. Baal is a "stripped" character— is man stripped of character. There is a paradox about the Victorian Man of Character, the Independent Individual of the age of individualism, which is that he was formed by that age and belonged utterly to that society. Conversely, the rejection of the individual that comes with the twentieth century, and especially after World War I, is a rejection of the society around him, and even of society as such. Baal is asocial man.

It would be natural enough to call him amoral, and his actions stamp him as what Freud called polymorphous

5

perverse: sensuality is acceptable to him in itself, and he does not limit himself to the "outlets" which society approves. However, if this were the beginning and end of Baal, the play that bears his name would simply be a tract favoring the noble savage, a return to an innocent paganism. Nothing could be further from the text before us. The image of an innocent paganism is present in it; but is by no means an image of the play as a whole. Baal beholds the innocence, the amorality, of Nature all around us, but he beholds it from a distance and with longing and envy. The *sky* would be an ideal mistress indeed, but how far off it is, how unreachable! Between us and primal innocence stands the world, which includes that very society of men which one would like to reject.

"Screw the world!" Those three syllables sum up a whole school of modern art and thought. Lautréamont had given the idea a homosexual form even earlier:

> Oh that the universe were an immense celestial anus! I would plunge my penis past its bloody sphincter, rending apart, with my impetuous motion, the very bones of the pelvis.

The prologue to *Baal* reads:

> And that girl the world, who gives herself and giggles
> If you only let her crush you with her thighs,
> Shared with Baal, who loved it, orgiastic wriggles.
> But he did not die. He looked her in the eyes.

No innocent enjoyment of beautiful Nature here! If Lautréamont is sadistic. Brecht is coolly defiant. He looks "that girl" in the eyes. How much lies behind such a look! How much pain and despair, how much living!

Though all drama tends to be about guilt, one might expect that a drama without individuals, without respect for society—a drama without ego or superego, one might be tempted to put it—would be an exception, would be "beyond guilt." One has read here and there that to give

6

up the individual is to give up the whole notion of responsibility. But it is not so, unless one is uttering a tautology, namely, that to give up the individual is to give up *individual* responsibility. Responsibility and guilt remain, and only seem the more unwieldy, the more oppressive, for not being neatly tied to this person and that action.

Brecht does make Baal seem cut off from the meaning of his own actions: from his killing of Ekart and his virtual killing of Johanna Reiher. Only with difficulty, looking back on the play, can one say to oneself: *it is a play about a murderer.* And yet by any humane standard murder is only one among Baal's several offenses and amid his consistent offensiveness. The immediate reason for this difficulty is to be found in Brecht's special perspective. He lends Baal a quality of innocence, but it is an innocence on the other side of guilt. Our minds, which are used to thinking here of a duality (guilt-innocence), have to stretch themselves a little to think in terms of three instead of two: innocence[1], guilt, and innocence[2]. This innocence[2] is the subject of much of Brecht's writing in this period. It could even be said that around 1919-1921 his favorite subject was the innocence that can accrue to extremely vicious, even extremely criminal, people. It is as if one were to speak of regained innocence in an old whore.

Dostoevsky, it could be added, does speak of such innocence. It is even inherent in Christianity, and was written out once for all in the New Testament story of Mary Magdalene. But Brecht's second innocence has no such authority behind it. It has no one's blessing except his own. It carries no "fringe benefits" in this world or the next. It is not a state of beatitude that endures, or that presages endurance. It is no more than a poet's feeling, an inspired hunch, a momentary dream, "just a thought": hence its peculiar pathos. If it holds out a hope, it is a hope neither of utopia here nor heaven there; it says merely that a life could be conceived of—at moments— that is not quite so bad.

7

> träumt er gelegentlich von einer kleinen Wiese
> mit blauem Himmel drüber und sonst nichts.

There *is* a dream of celestial bliss in Brecht's early work but it has the character of an ephemeral image, something that crosses the line of spiritual vision and is gone, a small loveliness sandwiched in between huge horrors. (Thus too, in a not so early work, the super-subtle lyric "Die Liebenden" is inserted in the story of *Mahagonny* between copulations that are paid for.) Insofar as Dostoevsky managed to believe in a real heaven, he could see it as transcending and swallowing up all that is unheavenly, even as eternity swallows up time. In Brecht it is hell—hell on earth—that is eternal, heaven that is swallowed up. The pathos of unbelief is pervasive in Brecht's life-work. It is his personal pathos, but is cogent and significant because it is also the characteristic pathos of the whole epoch.

For in the modern era, from Kierkegaard to Graham Greene, even the believers are not sure they really believe, they are only sure that they should. They are only able—like Brecht when later he came to "believe" in Communism—to "commit" themselves to a belief, i.e., take the consequences of joining the ranks of the faithful even though their faith is not really felt. Hence, *Baal* is genuine and solid whereas the Brecht plays that affirm Communism are, in that affirmation, spurious and factitious. *Baal* conveys the actual *Weltgefühl* of Bertolt Brecht throughout his career. A play like *Die Mutter* articulates the *Weltanschauung* which he agreed to commit himself to in the hope that a better *Welt* might come out of it after which the original *Weltgefühl* would change by itself. Even if this plan had all worked out, it would not make *Die Mutter* a better work of art than *Baal*; just the contrary. If all Brecht's later plays had been on the pattern of *Die Mutter*, his later works would simply have proved inferior to the earlier.

Brecht's "heaven" is momentary, and does not redeem: the guilt remains. And the guilt is all the greater for not

8

being only a guilt for specific offenses. When the individual disappears, what is left is the race. And the race is seen by Brecht as burdened with a primal curse—that which caused the Greeks to repeat that "not to be born is the best for man," and the Christians to formulate a doctrine of "original sin." If, at moments, we think that Brecht takes Baal's crimes too lightly—murder after all is murder—we quickly realize that in saying "Baal is no worse than the rest of us" he is not taking a high view of Baal but a low view of the rest of us. He is saying we are ourselves no better than murderers. We may even be worse than Baal, in that we may have missed the romance with the sky and the dream of the little meadow. We may be Baal minus the poetry.

And—what is partly the same thing—minus the pleasure. For though Baal's pleasures are ultimately poisoned by guilt and ended by aggression, they were not impure at the source. On the contrary, the search for pleasure is the one truly affirmative element in the play, and the reason why the poetry of the play retains a directly and even ingenuously romantic aura. Baal really was seeking

Immer das Land wo es besser zu leben ist.

More than thirty years later, Brecht was to take a look back at this play and speak of the love of pleasure, the search for happiness, as its subject. The comment is to be taken the more seriously in that *Baal* is, in all other respects, so unacceptable to the later Brecht. But the human longing for happiness "which cannot be killed" (as he put it) was a theme he was ready to pursue at all times. He reports that he tried to pick up the thread of *Baal* twenty years afterward in an opera libretto about a Chinese god of happiness. (True, he had come by then to believe that Russia was the "Land wo es besser zu leben ist" and that "Das Glück ist: der Kommunismus." With the early Brecht, it is as if he were striving to break through to a hedonism as radical as that of Herbert Marcuse or Norman

O. Brown. That guilt and anxiety blocked this path may, in one respect, have been fortunate: he was a dramatist— conflict was his raw material.)

In the fact that Baal is respected by Brecht as pleasure-seeker (though some readers may come to the play with an unfortunate puritanic prejudice) lies part of the reason that he is not pure villain. Walter Sokel has written of him eloquently as a parody of those Expressionistic heroes whose life was a sacred mission. But since Brecht considered the Expressionist missions spurious, he makes Baal's "mission" genuine. Baal is an ambiguous, ambivalent figure: part monster, but partly, too, the martyr of a poetic hedonism. And the positive element is more prominent than the negative because it is Baal's special contribution—his monstrousness he has in common with a monstrous world. (Later, the peculiar acidity of *The Threepenny Opera* would come from the implied proposition: "We on stage may be little crooks; but many of you out front are big ones.")

Yet if in the figure of Baal the more sympathetic element prevails over the less, in the play of *Baal* the poetry of life is overwhelmed by the prose, the beauty by the horror. If, as I believe, a good play amounts finally to a particular vision of life seen as a whole, then this play is a vision of life as an inferno, and the occasional faint gleam of beauty only makes the ugliness look more intensely black. Baal will let no one persuade him he has lost all chance of pleasure. But self is something he lost so long ago, its discovery is never on the cards. One might better put it that he never had a self. Whereas in Ibsen the self is threatened, and in Pirandello it is *said* not to exist, in Brecht both the Ibsenite self and the Pirandellian discussion are so far in the past they are totally forgotten. There remains the horror: Robert Lowell's "horror of the lost self." And this horror belongs even more to the play than to the protagonist.

"We possess nothing in the world—a mere chance can

strip us of everything—except the power to say *I*." So said Simone Weil. What then can a poet say for whom there is no *I* to affirm? "Nada y pues nada y nada y pues nada. Our nada, who are in nada, nada be thy name . . ." From Hemingway, in this famous passage published in 1933, to Samuel Beckett in the nineteen-fifties with his "nothing is more real than nothing," contemporary poets and poet-novelists and poet-dramatists have found themselves confronted and surrounded by nothingness. Brecht found himself in this situation in 1918 at the frighteningly youthful age of nineteen or twenty: "Das Schönste ist das Nichts." Googoo says this in the thirteenth scene of *Baal*. Brecht says it in every scene of *Baal*. Man, here, is alienated from the others and from himself, to the degree that both others and self may be said to non-exist, to be nothing. This idea—better, this sentiment, this lacerating conviction—gives a new poignancy to the old "ashes to ashes, dust to dust." If death, on the one hand, is an ironic ending to pleasure and beauty, it is, on the other, a direct, unironic continuation of the universal nothingness, the omnipresent death-in-life.

*Baal* is about nothingness. By that token it is also about death. Brecht might well have taken yet another idea from the playwright who most influenced him, Büchner, and called his play *Baal's Death*. The mythic Baal was a fertility god, hence a god of life. This mythological (i.e., unpsychological) drama presents the archetypal battle of life and death, Eros and Thanatos. Traditionally such a story would follow the pattern of rebirth: death followed by resurrection. Brecht who was always to parody the traditional patterns is doing so already in his first play where death is followed by . . . . death.

Some readers have found the play formless. What it finally achieves in the way of organic form must perhaps remain a matter of opinion but analysis will demonstrate at least that there is some very deliberate patterning here. For example, *Baal* is the play in which the protagonist

11

dies three times—in three ways that are poetically diversified. First, he dies as "Teddy," and speaks his own funeral oration (as Galy Gay is to do in *A Man's A Man*). Second, he relates his own death in the poem, "Death in the Forest." Third, there is his actual death scene, with which the play ends. The identity of the three deaths is clearly established by the identical forest setting and the identical cruel attitude of the dying one's fellow men. ("The coldness of the forests will be with me to my dying day," Brecht said in a famous poem; and he could have said the same of the coldness of those who are in attendance at the dying day—one thinks forward to the death of Swiss Cheese and, for that matter, the death of Brecht's Jesus in his "Song of the Hours.") Perhaps the whole play was planned as a kind of air and variations on the theme of dying. The drowning of Johanna is less an action than a leitmotif.

A final word on the Baal myth and Brecht's attitude to it. A writer from Augsburg, Brecht's native town, describes the poet's room at the time that he wrote Baal:

> . . . over the bed [was] a life-size picture of his idol Baal, that Semitic-Phoenician deity of insatiability which Christianity had declared the principle of evil. . . . Caspar Neher had drawn it in the then current style of Masereel after Brecht's model, a male vamp named K. from Pfersee near Augsburg.

> —Max Högel, *Bertolt Brecht, ein Porträt*

And this is probably to place the emphasis correctly: what would interest Brecht is that Baal was the enemy of the Christian-Judaic, puritanic, ascetic tradition. Perhaps he knew, too, that in the Canaanite *Poem of Baal* this god had an enemy, Môt, "the god," as Theodore Gaster says, "of all that lacks life and vitality"; the very name Môt means death. Standing for fertility, Baal was also the god of rainfall, and the association of fertility with

12

rain is something Brecht would remember when he created his comic fertility god—the Bloody Five of *A Man's A Man.*

Gaster's book *Thespis* reports many things which it is tempting to connect with Brecht's play, such as that the god Baal copulated with a calf, that "Baal's enveloping robe is . . . identified with the sky," and that, at his death, Baal "fell into the earth." In relation to the recurrent image of a corpse floating down a river, it is startling to read in Gaster that the motif is common in the folklore of Brecht's part of the world:

> In many of the seasonal mummeries representing the rout of the Dragon, or the expulsion of Death, Blight, or Winter, he is *flung into the water*. Thus, at Nuremberg, the traditional song specified that "we bear Death into the water". . . . At Tabor, Bohemia, it was said that "Death floats down the stream" . . . and at Bielsk, Podlachia, the effigy was drowned in a marsh or pond. . . . In Chrudim, Bohemia, Death was flung into the water on "Black Sunday" . . . [One of Brecht's early poems refers to Black Saturday] . . . In Silesia, children used to throw the effigy of Death into the river . . . while at Leipzig this was done by the local prostitutes and bastards. . . .

There is enough here to guarantee that Brecht's *Baal* will sooner or later be interpreted wholly in terms of myth and ritual. Such interpretations will be unbalanced —but less unbalanced than those that try to make sense of *Baal* on the lines of what was conventional drama in 1918.

Historians have shown that, in *Baal,* Brecht was mocking the Expressionists. Specifically, he sought to debunk Hanns Johst's image of the poet as ecstatic visionary amid the wicked materialism of the surrounding world. In effect, though, the young Brecht had taken on a much

13

larger antagonist than any Expressionist playwright. He had made a *tabula rasa* of the modern drama as a whole and on that bare surface had erected a primitive and already sturdy structure of his own. For better or for worse, a new era in dramatic art dates from this play.

—E.B.
September, 1963

# THE MODEL FOR BAAL

The dramatic biography *Baal* deals with the life of a man who actually existed. He was a certain Josef K. I heard stories about him from people who could distinctly remember not only him personally but also the sensation he created at the time. K. was the natural child of a washerwoman. He got himself a bad reputation quite early. Without any sort of education, he is supposed to have been capable of captivating even truly educated people with his astonishingly well-informed conversation. My friend told me he had made such an impression on a whole succession of fine young people with his incomparable deportment (his way of taking a cigarette, sitting down on a chair, and so on) that they took to imitating him. And yet he sank ever deeper through his heedless way of living, especially because—without ever taking the initiative—he shamelessly exploited every possibility that offered. Various shady episodes—the suicide of a young girl, for example—were laid to his account. He was a skillful mechanic but, so far as we know, never worked. When A. became too hot for him, he wandered rather far and wide with a medical student who'd seen better days, but then came back, in about 1911, to A. There this friend was stabbed to death in a tavern on the Lauterlech, almost certainly by K. himself. Anyhow, he forthwith fled and disappeared from A. and is supposed to have died miserably in the Black Forest.

—B.B., 1926

# BAAL

A play in twenty-one scenes

*by*

Bertolt Brecht

*English version by*

Eric Bentley and Martin Esslin

# CHARACTERS

BAAL, *a poet*
MECH, *publisher, big businessman*
MRS. MECH (EMILY)
DR. PILLER, *a critic*
JOHANNES SCHMIDT
JOHANNA, *fiancée of* JOHANNES
EKART, *a composer*
LOUISE, *a waitress*
TWO SISTERS
LANDLADY
SOPHIE BARGER
BUM
LUPU
MJURK, *owner of a nightspot*
CHANTEUSE
PIANIST
PARSON
BOLLEBOLL
GOOGOO
OLD BEGGAR
MAJA, *beggarwoman*
YOUNG WOMAN
WATZMANN
WAITRESS
TWO RANGERS
TEAMSTERS, FARMERS, LUMBERJACKS, *etc.*

*The Time*: About 1911
*The Place*: Augsburg and the surrounding region

19

# PROLOGUE

*Chorale of the Great Baal*

In the white womb of his mother Baal did lie.
Huge already, calm, and pallid was the sky,
Young and naked and immensely marvelous
As Baal loved it when Baal came to us.

And the sky stayed there in woe or glee
Even when Baal slept and smiled obliviously.
Nights, the sky was mauve; Baal drank a lot.
Mornings, Baal was good; sky, pale as apricot.

And through dive, cathedral, hospital, with ease
Baal jogs on toward the cure of the disease.
When Baal's tired, does he fall, my lads? Why, no,
Baal, he takes the sky with him below.

And where shameless sinners rolled in lawlessness
Nonchalantly wallowing, Baal lay.
Naught but sky to hide his nakedness!
(Hide it, though, all day and every day.)

And that girl the world, who gives herself and giggles
If you only let her crush you with her thighs,
Shared with Baal, who loved it, orgiastic wriggles.
But he did not die. He looked her in the eyes.

When Baal saw she was surrounded with the dead
Baal's delight was multiplied by three.
There is room, they're just a few, Baal said.
There is room, he said, above her knee.

If a woman gives you men her all
Let her go for she can give no more, says Baal.

As for other men, why, who fears men?
(Children, though, are something else again.)

Every vice, says Baal, is good for something.
It is vicious men who're good for nothing.
Vices can be worth a pretty penny.
Choose a couple, though! One is too many.

Don't be lazy! Have some fun or bust!
What you wish, says Baal, is what you must!
And your shit's your own, so sit and have a ball
Rather than do nothing, lads, at all!

Do not be so lazy and so soft, do not!
To enjoy oneself, says Baal, is hard, by God!
And you need strong limbs! Experience, too, they
say.
And a belly can be in the way.

Baal, he blinks at well-fed vultures overhead
Waiting up among the stars till Baal is dead.
Often Baal shams dead. So if the bird
Falls for this, Baal dines on vulture, sans a word.

In this vale of tears, and under gloomy stars,
Baal eats all the grass and smacks his lips.
When the fields are bare, Baal, singing, fares
Into the eternal forests where he sleeps.

When that girl the world begins to pull
Baal down into darkness, what is she to him? He's
full.
And beneath those eyelids Baal has sky to spare:
How could he use more now he lies there?

In the dark womb of the earth the rotting Baal did
lie.
Huge as ever, calm, and pallid was the sky,
Young and naked and immensely marvelous
As Baal loved it when Baal lived with us.

## SCENE 1

*Brightly lit room with table.* MECH, EMILY MECH, JO-HANNES, DR. PILLER, BAAL *enter.*

MECH: Care for a glass of wine?

*They sit down and eat.*

Do you eat crabmeat?

PILLER: You must publish your poems. Cekasack'll pay. He's a regular Maecenas. You'll get out of that attic.

MECH: Behold the corpse of an eel! I buy cinnamon wood. Whole forests of cinnamon wood drift down Brazilian rivers on my account. But I'll publish your poems, too.

EMILY: You live in an attic?

BAAL *eats and drinks.*

BAAL: Holzstrasse 64.

MECH: I am too fat for poetry, but you have a skull like a man I once loved in the Malayan archipelago. He used to have himself flogged to work. He could only work with bared teeth.

PILLER: Shall I write an essay about you? Do you have any manuscripts for me to look at? I have the backing of the press.

JOHANNES: Mr. Baal sings his poems to the teamsters. In a tavern by the river.

EMILY: More wine? But don't overdo it. Do you drink much? *(Fills his glass.)*

MECH: Do you travel? The sea—it's a purple wonder! Like to vomit into it sometime? And the Abyssinian mountains—they're something for you!

22

BAAL: They don't come to me.

PILLER: Your sense of life! Phew! Your songs have made quite an impact on me.

BAAL: The teamsters pay me for them if they like them.

MECH (*drinks*): I'll either publish your poems or let the cinnamon wood float away. Or both.

EMILY: You shouldn't drink so much.

BAAL: I have no shirts. I could use some white shirts.

MECH: You don't care for the publishing business?

BAAL: *Soft* shirts.

PILLER (*ironically*): And what do you think *I* could do for you?

EMILY: You make up such wonderful songs!

BAAL (*to* EMILY): Why not play something on the harmonium?

PILLER: What a porcupine you are!

MECH: I enjoy eating to harmonium music.

EMILY *plays.*

BAAL (*unbuttons his jacket; to* EMILY): You have good arms!

MECH: Have another eel. Pity to waste it, it would only swim into the latrines.

BAAL *pushes it back.*

No? Then, I'll eat it.

EMILY: Please don't drink too much, Mr. Baal.

BAAL (*looking at* EMILY): So cinnamon woods float down the rivers for you, Mech? Forests are felled for you? (*He goes on drinking all the time.*)

EMILY: You may drink as much as you wish. I only wanted to ask . . .

PILLER: Even as a drinker you are full of promise.

BAAL (*to* EMILY): You have good arms: one can see that now. Play so we can see those good arms!

EMILY *stops, goes to the table.*

PILLER: It isn't the *music* you like, is it?

BAAL: You talk too much: I don't even hear the music. But these arms are there to be seen.

MECH (*somewhat irritated*): Shall we make a bet who can eat more? I bet five muslin shirts, Baal.

BAAL: I've eaten enough. (*Looks at* EMILY.)

PILLER: Your poetry has something evil about it. That, I'm afraid, is certain.

BAAL: Don't you trade in animals, too, Mech?

MECH: Got anything against that? May I have your poems?

BAAL (*stroking* EMILY'S *arm*): What business of yours are my poems?

MECH: I wanted to do you a good turn. Emily, won't you peel a few more apples?

PILLER: He's afraid of being exploited. You've still not figured how I might be useful to you?

BAAL: Always wear wide sleeves, Emily.

EMILY: You must stop drinking that wine.

MECH: Don't you want to take a bath? Shall I have a bed made up for you? Haven't you forgotten something?

PILLER: The shirts are floating away, Baal. The poems *have* floated away.

BAAL (*to* EMILY): I live on Holzstrasse, number 64. Why shouldn't you sit on my knee? Aren't your thighs trembling under your skirt? (*Drinks.*) Why monopolies? Go to bed, Mech!

MECH (*has got up*): I like all the animals the Lord created. But this is an animal one can't do business with. Come on, Emily! Come on, Piller! Come on, Johannes! (*Exit.*)

PILLER (*on the way to the door*): Dead drunk!

BAAL (*to* JOHANNES): What is the gentleman's name?

JOHANNES: Piller. (*Standing, puts his arm around* BAAL'S *shoulder.*)

BAAL: Piller! *You* can send me some used newspapers!

PILLER (*leaving the room*): For me you don't exist. (*Exit.*)

JOHANNES (*to* BAAL): May I visit you in your attic? May I go home with you? Is there anything you still want from him, Mrs. Mech?

EMILY (*in the door*): I am sorry for him.

BAAL *sits alone, goes on drinking.*

BAAL'S *attic.*

*Starlit night. At the window* BAAL *and the youth* JO-
HANNES. *They see sky.*

BAAL: When you lie stretched out in the grass at night
you feel in your bones that the earth is a sphere and
that we are flying and that there are animals on this
star eating up the plants. It is one of the smaller
stars.

JOHANNES: You know something of astronomy?

BAAL: No.

*Silence.*

JOHANNES: I have a mistress. She is the most innocent
thing alive, but, in a dream once, I saw her mating
with a holly tree: her white body lay stretched out
on the holly tree, and the bulbous branches held her
in their embrace. I haven't been able to sleep since.

BAAL: Have you looked at her white body yet?

JOHANNES: No. She is innocent. Even her knees . . .
there are many degrees of innocence, aren't there?
And yet, sometimes, at night, when I hold her in
my arms for a moment, she trembles like a leaf. But
only at night. But I am too weak to go through with
it. She is seventeen.

BAAL: And love—did she enjoy it in your dream?

JOHANNES: Yes.

BAAL: She has white underwear round her body, a snow-
white slip between her knees? After you've slept
with her, she may be a heap of flesh without a face.

26

JOHANNES: I've always felt that. I thought I was a coward. You agree, don't you: the union of bodies is a filthy thing?

BAAL: That's just the grunting of the pigs who can't make it! When you clasp those virgin hips, in the fear and ecstasy of a created being, you will become God. Just as the holly tree has many roots, all entwined together, so the two of you in the one bed have many limbs, and your hearts beat in your breasts and the blood flows in your veins.

JOHANNES: But the law punishes it. As do parents.

BAAL: Your parents (*He reaches for his guitar.*) are a thing of the past. Rotting teeth in their mouths. How can they open such mouths against love, which can be the death of any of us? If love is too much for you, you vomit yourselves up. (*He is tuning the guitar.*)

JOHANNES: She gets pregnant, you mean?

BAAL (*with some harsh chords*): When summer swims off, mild and pale, they have already sucked up love like sponges, and they've turned back into animals, childish and wicked, with fat bellies and dripping breasts, completely shapeless, and with wet, clinging arms like slimy squids. And their bodies disintegrate, and are sick unto death. And with a ghastly outcry, as if a new world were on the way, they give birth to a small piece of fruit. They spit out in torment what once they had sucked up in lust. (*He plays glissandos.*) One must have teeth. Then love's like biting into an orange when the juice squirts in your teeth.

JOHANNES: *Your* teeth are the teeth of an animal: grayish-yellow, massive, uncanny.

BAAL: And love's like letting your naked arm drift in pond water with weeds between your fingers. Like torment at which a drunken tree, when the wild winds ride it, starts singing with a groan. Like

27

drowning in gurgling wine on a hot day. And her
body seeps like very cool wine into every fold of
your skin. Your joints are pliable as plants in the
wind. And the force of the attack is so great, you
feel you're flying against a stormwind. You give
way, and her body rolls over you like cool gravel.
But love is also like a coconut which is good while
it's fresh, but you have to spit it out when the juice
is gone, what's left tastes bitter. (*Throws the guitar
away.*) But enough of this aria.

JOHANNES: So you think I should go ahead, if it's so
beautiful?

BAAL: I think *you* should steer clear, my dear Johannes.

# SCENE 3

*Bar room.*

*Morning.* BAAL. TEAMSTERS. *In the back* EKART *with the waitress,* LOUISE. *Through the window a glimpse of white clouds.*

BAAL (*telling his story to the* TEAMSTERS): He threw me out of his white rooms because I spat out his wine. But his wife ran after me and in the evening we had quite a time. Now I've got her on my neck and I'm sick of her.

TEAMSTERS: She deserves a good spanking. They're as horny as mares but not as bright. She should eat plums! I always beat mine black and blue before I give it to her.

JOHANNES *enters with* JOHANNA.

JOHANNES: This is Johanna.

BAAL (*to the* TEAMSTERS *who are going upstage*): I'll come and join you at the back and sing to you later. Hi, Johanna.

JOHANNA: Johannes has read me some of your songs.

BAAL: Is that so? How old are you?

JOHANNES: She was seventeen last June.

JOHANNA: I'm jealous of you. He always speaks of you with such enthusiasm.

BAAL: You're in love with your Johannes. It's spring now. I'm waiting for Emily. Love is better than mere pleasure.

JOHANNES: I can understand that *men's* hearts warm to you, but how could you succeed with women?

29

EMILY *enters quickly*.

BAAL: Here she is. Morning, Emily. Johannes has
brought his fiancée. Sit down.

EMILY: How can you ask me here? A lot of riffraff in a
low-down dive! So this is your taste.

BAAL: Louise, a shot for the lady!

EMILY: You want to make me look ridiculous?

BAAL: No. You'll drink. We're all human.

EMILY: *You're* not.

BAAL: You should know. (*Holds the glass out to
LOUISE.*) Not such short measure, virgin. (*Embraces
her.*) You are so damned soft today! Like a plum.

EMILY: What bad taste!

BAAL: Shout even louder, my love!

JOHANNES: At any rate, it's interesting here. Simple
people. How they drink and joke! And then—the
clouds through the window!

EMILY: I suppose he's dragged you here too? To the
white clouds?

JOHANNA: Shouldn't we go down to the river instead,
Johannes?

BAAL: Nothing of the sort! You stay here! (*Drinks.*)
The sky is purple, specially when one's drunk. Beds,
on the other hand, are white. Beforehand. There is
love here, between the sky and the soil. (*Drinks.*)
Why are you such cowards? The sky's wide open,
you little shadows! Full of bodies! Pale from loving!

EMILY: You've drunk too much again, so you jabber.
And with a fascinating line of talk he drags you to
his trough.

BAAL: The sky— (*Drinks.*) is also yellow sometimes.
With birds of prey in it. You must get drunk. (*Looks
under the table.*) Who's kicking my shins? Is it you,
Louise? Oh it's you, Emily! Well, never mind. Just
have a drink!

EMILY (*who has half risen*): I don't know what's the

30

matter with you today. Maybe I shouldn't have come here after all.

BAAL: You see that now? Now you can stay.

JOHANNA: You shouldn't do this, Mr. Baal.

BAAL: You have a kind heart, Johanna. When the time comes, you won't deceive your husband, hm?

TEAMSTER (*bursts out*): Trumps, you pig! My trick!

SECOND TEAMSTER: Go on, says the gal, we almost made it!

*Laughter.*

They should eat plums!

THIRD TEAMSTER: "You should be ashamed of such infidelity," said the lady to the hired man who slept with the maid.

*Laughter.*

JOHANNES (*to* BAAL): . . . for Johanna's sake, she's still a child!

JOHANNA (*to* EMILY): Like to come with me? We could leave together.

EMILY (*sobbing, crouched over the table*): Now I'm ashamed.

JOHANNA (*putting her arm round her*): I understand. Don't fret.

EMILY: Don't look at me like that! You are so very young. You know nothing yet.

BAAL (*rises in a dark mood*): A comedy entitled: Sisters of the Under-world. (*Goes to the* TEAMSTERS, *takes the guitar from the wall and tunes it.*)

JOHANNA: He's had too much to drink, dear lady. To-morrow he'll be sorry.

EMILY: If you only knew: he's always like that. And I love him.

BAAL (*sings*):

Orge said to me:

The dearest place on earth was not (he'd say)
The grassy plot where his dead parents lay:

Nor a confessional nor harlot's bed
Nor a soft lap, warm, white, and fat (he said).

The place which he liked best to look upon
In this wide world of ours was the john.

It is a place where you rejoice to know
That there are stars above and dung below.

A place where you can sit—a wondrous sight—
And be alone even on your wedding night.

A place that teaches you (so Orge sings):
Be humble, for you can't hold on to things!

A place where one can rest and yet where one
Gently but firmly can get business done.

A place of wisdom where one has the leisure
To get one's paunch prepared for future pleasure.

And there you find out what you are indeed:
A fellow who sits on a john to—feed!

TEAMSTERS (*applauding*): Bravo!—Great song!—A
sherry brandy for Mr. Baal, if he'll accept it—And
all his own work!—I take my hat off to that!

LOUISE (*in the middle of the room*): You are a naughty
man, Mr. Baal.

FIRST TEAMSTER: If you took up something useful, you'd
get somewhere. Later on, you might own a trans-
port business.

SECOND TEAMSTER: A head like that. A man could *use*
a head like that.

BAAL: Don't overrate the head. You need a backside too
and all that goes with it. Your health, Louise!

32

*(Returns to his table.)* Your health, Emmy! Go on, drink at least, if you can't do anything else! Drink, I tell you!

EMILY, *with tears in her eyes, takes a small sip from the brandy glass.*

That's right. Now there'll be some fire in you!

EKART *has got up, slowly comes toward* BAAL *from behind the counter. He is haggard and a big fellow.*

EKART: Baal! Let all that go! Come with me, brother! To the roads with their hard-caked dust and the air turning purple toward evening. To the dives full of drunks. The women you have filled with your seed tumble into the black rivers. To the cathedrals with little white women. You'll say: is one allowed to breathe here? To the cowsheds where you sleep among the animals. They are dark and full of mooing. And to the forests: an iron clangor above and you forget the light of the sky: God has forgotten *you.* Do you remember what the sky looks like? You've become an operatic tenor. *(Opens his arms wide.)* Come with me, brother! Dancing and music and liquor! Rain soaking you to the skin! Sun burning your skin! Darkness and light! Women and dogs! Have you run to seed already?

BAAL: Louise, an anchor! Don't leave me alone with this man.

LOUISE *moves toward him.*

Come, help me, children!

JOHANNES: Don't let yourself be seduced!

BAAL: Call me Parsifal.

JOHANNES: Think of your mother and your art! Be strong! *(To* EKART:*)* You ought to be ashamed of yourself. You are the devil.

EKART: Come, brother Baal. Like two white doves, let

33

us blissfully fly into the blue. Rivers in the light of dawn! Cemeteries in the wind! The smell of the endless fields before they are mown!

JOHANNA: Be steadfast, Mr. Baal!

EMILY (*presses herself against him*): You mustn't! Do you hear me? You are too good for that!

BAAL: It's too soon, Ekart! There are still other ways! They won't come with me, brother!

EKART: Then go to hell. With your child's head and your fat heart. (*Exit.*)

TEAMSTERS: Let's see the ten of diamonds!—Hell!—Let's count!—Finished!

JOHANNA: This time you've won, Mr. Baal.

BAAL: I'm sweating. Are you free tonight, Louise?

EMILY: Don't talk like that, Baal. You don't realize what you're doing to me.

LOUISE: Let madam be, Mr. Baal. Any child can see she's out of her mind.

BAAL: Be quiet, Louise. Horgauer!

FIRST TEAMSTER: What is it?

BAAL: There's a woman here being maltreated. She wants love. Give her a kiss, Horgauer.

JOHANNES: Baal!

JOHANNA *puts her arms round* EMILY.

TEAMSTERS (*beating the table, laughing*): Come on, Andrew!—Take her!—A fine lady! Blow your nose first, Andrew.—You're an animal, Mr. Baal.

BAAL: Are you cold, Emily? Do you love me? He's bashful, Emmy. Kiss him. If you let me down in front of these people, we're through. One. Two.

TEAMSTER *bends down*. EMILY *lifts her tear-stained face toward him him; he gives her a loud kiss. Loud laughter.*

JOHANNES: That was wicked, Baal! Drinking brings out

34

the bad in him and then he feels good. He's too strong.

TEAMSTERS: Good for him! What does she go to dives for! That's how a man should act.—She's an adulteress!—She had it coming! (*They make ready to leave.*) She should eat plums!

JOHANNA: You ought to be ashamed.

BAAL (*going near her*): How is it your knees are trembling, Johanna?

JOHANNES: What do you want?

BAAL (*his hand on his shoulder*): What do you have to write poems for? When life's so decent: if you drift down a fast-flowing river, naked, on your back under an orange-colored sky, and you see nothing but the sky as it turns purple and later black like a hole . . . if you trample an enemy into the dust . . . or turn sorrow into music . . . or cry for unrequited love and eat an apple . . . or bend a woman's body over a bed . . .

JOHANNES *silently leads* JOHANNA *out of the room.*

(*Bending over the table.*) Did you feel it? Did it pierce your skin? A circus! You have to lure the animal into the open! Out into the sun with the beast! The check please! Out into the daylight with love! Naked in the sun beneath the sky!

TEAMSTERS (*they shake his hand*): So long, Mr. Baal! —Our respects, Mr. Baal.—You see, Mr. Baal: I for my part always reckoned Mr. Baal wasn't quite right in the head. With his songs and all. But this is for sure: your heart's in the right place!—Women must be treated right.—Well, today, there were some white buttocks on show here.—A good morning to you, Mr. Circus! (*Exeunt.*)

BAAL: Good morning, my friends.

EMILY *has thrown herself across the bench, sobbing.*

BAAL *strokes her forehead with the back of his hand.*

Emmy, you can be quiet now. Now it's behind you. (*Lifts her face up, brushes her hair from her wet face.*) Forget it! (*Throws himself heavily on her, and kisses her.*)

BAAL'S *attic.*

*I. Dawn.* BAAL *and* JOHANNA *sitting on the edge of the bed.*

JOHANNA: Oh, what have I done? I am bad.

BAAL: You'd better wash.

JOHANNA: I still don't know how it happened.

BAAL: It's Johannes' fault. Brings you up here and then fades out of the picture when it dawns on him why your knees are trembling.

JOHANNA (*getting up, in a softer voice*): If he came back . . .

BAAL: Idiot! I am fed up, my love. (*Lies down again.*) The dawn rising on Mount Ararat.

JOHANNA: Shall I get up?

BAAL: After the flood. Stay in bed.

JOHANNA: Don't you want to open the window?

BAAL: I love the smell.—How about another helping? Gone is gone.

JOHANNA: How coarse you can be!

BAAL (*lazily on the bed*): White and washed clean by the flood, Baal lets his thoughts soar over the black waters like doves.

JOHANNA: Where's my bodice? I can't, like that . . .

BAAL (*holding it out to her*): Here!—What can't you, my love . . . ?

JOHANNA: Go home. (*Drops the bodice, but then puts it on.*)

BAAL (*whistling*): A wild bumblebee! I can feel each of my bones separately. Give me a kiss!

JOHANNA (*by the table, in the center of the room*): Say something!

BAAL *remains silent.*

Do you still love me? Tell me.

BAAL *whistles.*

Can't you say it?

BAAL (*contemplating the ceiling*): I'm fed to the teeth.

JOHANNA: Then what was it last night? And just now?

BAAL: Johannes is capable of making a fuss. Emily is still running around like a sailboat with a hole in the water line. And I can starve to death here. None of you will lift a finger to help me. You all only want one thing.

JOHANNA (*confusedly clearing the table*): And you never felt differently about me?

BAAL: Have you washed? No practical sense at all! Didn't you get anything out of it? Then go! Go home! You can tell Johannes that I took you home last night and that I spit bile at him. It's been raining. (*Pulls the blanket round him.*)

JOHANNA: Johannes? (*Moves heavily to the door. Exits.*)

BAAL (*turning round sharply*): Johanna! (*Jumps out of bed, to the door:*) Johanna! (*At the window:*) Just watch her run! Watch her run! (*He wants to go back to bed, but then throws a cushion on the floor and sinks down on it with a groan.*)

It's growing dark. A hurdygurdy is heard from the courtyard.


II. Noon. BAAL *lying on the bed.*


BAAL (*singing softly*):

Carousing makes the evening sky
Turn purple, brown, and black.
Spoiling for the fight you lie
Flat upon your back.

*The* TWO SISTERS *enter, arm in arm.*

ELDER SISTER: You said we should come and visit you
again.

BAAL (*goes on singing*): In a bed both broad and
white . . .

ELDER SISTER: We've come, Mr. Baal.

BAAL: Now they flutter into the dovecote in pairs. . . .
Undress!

ELDER SISTER: Last week mother heard a noise on the
stairs. (*She opens her sister's blouse.*)

YOUNGER SISTER: It was already pretty dusky on the
stairs when we crept up to the attic.

BAAL: One day I'll have you on my neck.

YOUNGER SISTER: I'd drown myself, Mr. Baal.

ELDER SISTER: There are two of us. . . .

YOUNGER SISTER: I'm ashamed, sister.

ELDER SISTER: It isn't the first time.

YOUNGER SISTER: But it's never been so light, sister. High
noon.

ELDER SISTER: It isn't the second time, either. . . .

YOUNGER SISTER: You must undress, too.

ELDER SISTER: I'll undress in a minute.

BAAL: When you're ready, you can come to me. Then it'll
get dark.

YOUNGER SISTER: Today *you've* got to be first, sister.

ELDER SISTER: I was first last time.

YOUNGER SISTER: No, it was me. . . .

BAAL: Both come at the same time.

ELDER SISTER (*standing, her arms round the younger
sister*): We're ready. It's so light in here.

BAAL: Is it warm outside?

ELDER SISTER: It's only April.

39

YOUNGER SISTER: But the sun is warm outside today.

BAAL: Did you like it last time?

*Silence.*

ELDER SISTER: A girl has drowned herself: Johanna Reiher.

YOUNGER SISTER: In the river Laach. I wouldn't drown myself there. It flows so fast.

BAAL: Drowned herself? Do they know why?

ELDER SISTER: People are talking. It gets around.

YOUNGER SISTER: She left home in the evening and stayed away all night.

BAAL: She didn't go back home in the morning?

YOUNGER SISTER: No, she drowned herself. But they haven't found her yet.

BAAL: Still floating . . .

YOUNGER SISTER: What's the matter, sister?

ELDER SISTER: Maybe I was cold for a moment.

BAAL: I'm so lazy today. You can go home.

ELDER SISTER: You mustn't do that, Mr. Baal. You mustn't do that to her!

*A knock at the door.*

YOUNGER SISTER: Someone knocked. That's mother.

ELDER SISTER: For God's sake, don't open!

YOUNGER SISTER: I'm afraid, sister.

ELDER SISTER: Your blouse!

*More insistent knocking.*

BAAL: If this is your mother, it's up to you to talk yourself out of it.

ELDER SISTER (*dressing quickly*): Wait a little before you open: bolt the door, for God's sake!

*The fat LANDLADY enters.*

LANDLADY: Well, well, just look, I thought so! Two at a

time now! Aren't you ashamed of yourselves? Together in this man's pond? From morning to night
and again till morning his bed never gets cold. But
now I have a word to say: my attic isn't a brothel.

BAAL *turns his face to the wall.*

I suppose you're sleepy? Well, can you never have
too much woman flesh? You're so worn out, the
sun shines right through you. There's nothing but
skin on your bones.

BAAL (*with a movement of his arms*): They flutter into
my grove like swans!

LANDLADY (*clapping her hands together*): Pretty swans!
Your language! You could become a poet, you really
could! If your knees don't rot off.

BAAL: I gorge myself on white bodies.

LANDLADY: White bodies! You *are* a poet! You're nothing
else, anyway! And those young things! I suppose
you're sisters? Maybe you're orphans: you want to
drown us in tears. Shall I give you a beating? On
those "white bodies"?

BAAL *laughs.*

And *you* laugh? Corrupting poor girls by the ton!
Luring them into your cave? Fie on you! I hereby
give you notice. Now move on, you two, and go
home to mother, I'll come with you!

*The* YOUNGER SISTER *cries more violently.*

ELDER SISTER: It's not her fault, lady.

LANDLADY (*taking both by the hand*): So it's raining, is
it? Such people! Well, you're not the only ones who
come here. He buys swans wholesale. He made
quite a lot of swans happy, and then threw their
empty skins on the dung-heap. So get out into the
good clean air! No need of saltwater here! (*Takes
both girls round the shoulders.*) I know what he's

like! I know his trademark. Don't weep right away, people will notice. Just go quietly home to mother and don't do it again. (*Pushing them toward the door.*) And you: I'm giving you notice! You can install your swannery elsewhere! (*Pushes the two girls out. Exit.*)

BAAL (*gets up, stretches*): A hag with a heart!—I felt damned lazy today anyway. (*Throws paper on the table, sits down in front of it.*) I'll turn over a new leaf. (*Sketches large initials on the paper.*) I'll give my inner man a try. I'm quite hollowed out. But ravenous as a beast of prey. Nothing but skin on my bones. The hag! (*Leans back, stretching arms and legs, emphatically.*) Now I'll make the summer. Red. Scarlet. Greedy. (*He starts humming again.*)

*It turns dark again. Then the hurdygurdy is heard.*


*III. Evening.* BAAL *is sitting at the table.*


BAAL (*clasping the brandy bottle; intermittently*): It's the fourth day I've spent spattering summer on this paper: wild, pale, greedy. And I keep fighting the brandy bottle. There have been defeats, but now the bodies are starting to fall back to the walls, into Egyptian darkness. I beat them all back to the wooden walls. Only I mustn't drink any brandy. (*He gabbles.*) Pale brandy is my stick and my staff. Since the snow started dripping from the gutter, my untouched paper has been mirrored in the brandy bottles. But now my hands are trembling. As though they were still holding bodies. (*He listens.*) My heart's beating like a horse's hoof. (*He muses romantically.*) Oh, Johanna, another night in your aquarium and I'd have rotted away among the fish.

But now the odor of the mild nights of May is in me. I am a lover without a mistress. I'm losing the battle. (*He drinks, gets up.*) I have to move out. But first I'll get myself a woman. To move out by oneself is sad. (*Looking out of the window:*) Anyone. With a face like a woman. (*Exit, humming.*)

*Downstairs a harmonium is heard, playing Tristan. JOHANNES, gone to seed and pale, enters by the door. Rummages among the papers on the table. Lifts the bottle. Shyly to the door, where he waits.*

*Noise on the stairs. Whistling.*

BAAL *drags* SOPHIE BARGER *in; whistles.*

BAAL: Be nice to me, my love! This is my room. (*Makes her sit down. Notices* JOHANNES:) What are *you* doing here?

JOHANNES: I only wanted . . .

BAAL: Is that so? You only wanted? Just standing around? A tombstone for my late Johanna? Johannes, a corpse from another world, is that it? I'll throw you out! Out with you this minute! (*Runs round him.*) It's an impertinence! I'll bang you against the wall, it's spring anyway. Jump!

JOHANNES *looks at him. Exits.*

BAAL *whistles.*

SOPHIE BARGER: What has that young man done to you? Let me go!

BAAL (*opens the door wide*): One floor down, then turn right.

SOPHIE BARGER: They ran after us, when you suddenly lifted me up, down there in front of the doorway. They'll find me.

BAAL: No one'll find you here.

SOPHIE BARGER: I don't know you. What do you want with me?

43

BAAL: If you ask such questions, you can go away again.

SOPHIE BARGER: You attacked me in the street. I thought it was an orangutan.

BAAL: After all, it's spring. I had to have something white in this damned cavern! A cloud! (*Opens the door, listens.*) These fools have gone.

SOPHIE BARGER: I'll be thrown out of the house if I get home late.

BAAL: Particularly looking like that.

SOPHIE BARGER: Looking like what?

BAAL: As one looks when one has been made love to by me.

SOPHIE BARGER: I don't know why I'm still here.

BAAL: I can enlighten you.

SOPHIE BARGER: Please don't think anything bad of me!

BAAL: Why not? You're a woman like any other. The face is different. Their knees are all weak.

SOPHIE BARGER *half wants to go, turns round at the door.* BAAL *looks at her, sitting astride a chair.*

SOPHIE BARGER: Good-bye!

BAAL (*calmly*): You seem to have difficulty breathing?

SOPHIE BARGER: I don't know, I'm feeling so weak. (*She leans against the wall.*)

BAAL: I know. It's April. It's getting dark and you can smell me. That's how it goes with the animals. (*Rises.*) And now you belong to the wind, my white cloud! (*Quickly toward her, bangs the door to, takes* SOPHIE BARGER *in his arms.*)

SOPHIE BARGER (*out of breath*): Let me go!

BAAL: My name is Baal.

SOPHIE BARGER: Let me go!

BAAL: You must comfort me. I was weak from the winter. And you look like a woman.

SOPHIE BARGER (*looks up to him*): Your name is Baal?

BAAL: Don't you want to go home?

44

SOPHIE BARGER (*looking up to him*): You are so ugly, so ugly a girl is frightened. . . . But then . . .

BAAL: Hm?

SOPHIE BARGER: Then it doesn't matter.

BAAL (*kisses her*): You've got strong knees, huh?

SOPHIE BARGER: Do you know my name? My name is Sophie Barger.

BAAL: You must forget it. (*Kisses her.*)

SOPHIE BARGER: Don't . . . Don't . . . Do you know that nobody ever yet . . .

BAAL: Are you a virgin? Come! (*He leads her to the bed, upstage. They sit down.*) You see: in this wooden attic cascades of bodies have lain. But now I want a face. In the night we'll go outside. We'll lie down among flowers and trees. You are a woman. I have become unclean. You must love me for a time.

SOPHIE BARGER: You're like this, are you? . . . I do love you.

BAAL (*lays his head against her breast*): Now there's sky above us and we are alone.

SOPHIE BARGER: But you must lie still.

BAAL: Like a child!

SOPHIE BARGER (*raises herself up*): My mother—at home —I must go home.

BAAL: Is she old?

SOPHIE BARGER: She is seventy.

BAAL: Then she's used to wickedness.

SOPHIE BARGER: And if the earth swallows me up? If I'm dragged into a cavern one evening and I never return?

BAAL: Never?

*A silence.*

Do you have brothers and sisters?

SOPHIE BARGER: Yes. They need me.

BAAL: The air in this room is like milk. (*Gets up. At the window:*) The willows by the river are dripping wet

45

and disheveled from the rain. (*Grasps her.*) You must have pale thighs.

*It gets dark again and the hurdygurdy is heard again from the courtyard.*

*Whitewashed houses and brown tree trunks. Dark bells.*

BAAL. *The* BUM, *a pale, drunken individual.*

BAAL (*circling round the* BUM *who is sitting on a stone, his pale face turned upward*): Who has nailed the corpses of the trees to the walls?*

BUM: The pale, ivory-colored air around the corpses of trees: Corpus Christi.

BAAL: And bells for good measure, when the vegetation is dying!

BUM: As for me, the bells are edifying.

BAAL: Don't the trees depress you?

BUM: Ah! the dead bodies of trees! (*Takes a sip from a brandy flask.*)

BAAL: The bodies of women are no better!

BUM: What connection have the bodies of women with the Corpus Christi procession?

BAAL: They are filth! You are not in love!

BUM: I love the white body of Jesus! (*Hands the bottle up to him.*)

BAAL (*mellower*): I have songs here on this paper. But now they're going to be hung in the toilet.

BUM (*transfigured*): To serve! To serve my Lord Jesus: I see the white body of Jesus. Jesus loved evil.

BAAL (*drinks*): As I do.

BUM: Do you know the story about him and the dead dog? They all said: "It's stinking carrion! Send for

* Trees are set up outside the houses at Corpus Christi. (E.B., M..E.)

47

the police! One can't stand it!" But he said: "It has beautiful white teeth."

BAAL: Perhaps I'll turn Catholic.

BUM: *He* didn't. (*Takes the bottle back.*)

BAAL (*again running around, indignantly*): But the bodies of women which he nails to the wall, I wouldn't do that.

BUM: Nailed to the walls! They didn't drift down rivers, they were slaughtered for him, the white body of Jesus.

BAAL (*takes the bottle from him, turns away*): You have either too much religion or too much brandy inside you. (*Exits with the bottle.*)

BUM (*losing all control, shouts after him*): So you don't want to stand by your ideals, Sir! You don't want to hurl yourself into the procession! You love trees but don't want to help them?

BAAL: I'm going down to the river to wash. I don't care for corpses. (*Exit.*)

BUM: But I have brandy inside me, I can't stand it, I can't stand these damned dead trees. If one had a lot of brandy inside one, maybe one could stand it.

*A night in May: under some trees.*

BAAL. SOPHIE.

BAAL (*lazily*): Now the rain has stopped. The grass must still be wet . . . the water didn't penetrate our leaves . . . the young leaves are dripping, but here, among the roots, it is dry. (*Angrily.*) Why can't one sleep with trees?

SOPHIE: Listen!

BAAL: The wild rushing of the wind in the wet, black foliage! Can you hear the rain dripping through the leaves?

SOPHIE: I can feel one drop on my neck. . . . Oh, Baal, let me go!

BAAL: The whirlpool of love tears the clothes off one's back and, after one has seen the sky, buries one, naked, under the corpses of leaves.

SOPHIE: I should like to hide myself in you because I'm naked, Baal.

BAAL: I am drunk and you are reeling. The sky is black, and we are on a swing with love inside us, and the sky is black. I love you.

SOPHIE: Oh Baal! My mother's crying about my death. She thinks I've gone and got drowned. How many weeks is it now? It wasn't even May yet. Maybe three weeks.

BAAL: Three weeks, says the loved one in the roots of the trees, when it was thirty years. And at that very moment she had rotted half away.

SOPHIE: It is good to lie this way like some robber's loot, and the sky is above you, and you'll never be alone again.

BAAL: Now I'll take your slip off again.

49

*Night Cloud, a nightspot.*

*A small filthy café, whitewashed dressing room, in the back left a dark brown curtain, to the right the whitewashed wooden door to the toilet; at the back right a door. When it is open, you can see the blue night. In the café in the back a* CHANTEUSE *is singing.*

BAAL *walking around with a bare chest, drinking, humming.*

LUPU, *a fat, pallid youth with black, shiny hair, in two strands pasted onto his sweaty pale forehead, his head pointed at the back.*

LUPU (*in the door, right*): Someone's knocked the lamp over again.

BAAL: Only pigs come here. Where's my shot of brandy again?

LUPU: You've drunk it all.

BAAL: You be careful.

LUPU: Mr. Mjurk said something about a sponge.

BAAL: So I get no brandy?

LUPU: Before the performance, there will be no more brandy for you, says Mr. Mjurk. As for me, I'm sorry for you.

MJURK (*through the curtain*): Off with you, Lupu!

BAAL: I must get my brandy, Mjurk, or there'll be no poetry.

MJURK: You shouldn't drink so much, or one night you won't be able to sing at all.

BAAL: What's the point of singing, anyhow?

50

MJURK: You and the chanteuse Savettka are the most
brilliant numbers at the Night Cloud. I've discovered you with my own hands. When was such a
tender soul buried in such a hunk of fat before? It's
the hunk of fat that brings success, not the poetry.
Your brandy-swilling will ruin me.

BAAL: I'm tired of fighting every night about my con-
tractual brandy. I'm going.

MJURK: I have the backing of the police. Try a good
night's sleep sometime. As a change, my good man.
You totter about as though your knee tendons were
cut. Get rid of your mistress!

*Applause from the café.*

You're on.

BAAL: I'm fed to the teeth.

*The CHANTEUSE, with the PIANIST, a pale, lethargic
individual, enters through the curtain.*

CHANTEUSE: Time to lay off!

MJURK (*pressing a frock coat on BAAL*): One doesn't go
on stage half-naked in my establishment.

BAAL *throws the frock coat away and exits, dragging
his guitar behind him, through the curtain.*

CHANTEUSE (*sits down, drinks*): He's only working for
his girl. He lives with her. He's a genius. Lupu
copies him shamelessly. He's adopted the same tone
of voice. And the same girl.

PIANIST (*leaning against the toilet door*): His songs are
divine, but he's been squabbling with Lupu about
his brandy ration for the last eleven nights.

CHANTEUSE (*drinks*): We're a miserable lot.

BAAL (*behind the curtain*):

Who so pure as little me?
I run through life so cheerfully.

51

*Applause.*

*He continues, with guitar.*

The wind, it howled through every street.
The child had big blue plums to eat.
And it also, every night,
Played with its body so soft and white.

*Applause in the café, with some cries of protest.*
BAAL *continues to sing. The turmoil increases, as
the song becomes more and more shameless. Finally,
there is an immense row in the café.*

PIANIST (*apathetically*): Hell! He's running out! Ambulance! Now Mjurk's talking, but they're tearing him apart. He's given them the whole story quite raw.

BAAL *enters through the curtain, dragging his guitar.*

MJURK (*behind him*): You animal, I'll get you for this. You'll sing your number! It's in the contract! Or I call the police! (*He returns to the auditorium.*)
PIANIST: You're ruining us, Baal.

BAAL *grasps his own throat, goes right to the toilet
door.*

PIANIST (*does not make way*): Where do you want to go?

BAAL *pushes him away, exits through the door, with
the guitar.*

CHANTEUSE: Taking the guitar to the john with you? You are divine!
MEMBERS OF THE AUDIENCE (*putting their heads through
the curtain*): Where is the pig?—Go on singing!—
What a pig! (*They withdraw.*)
MJURK (*enters*): I talked to them like a Salvation Army major. We can count on the police. But these people

52

are clamoring for him again. Where is the fellow? He must go on stage.

PIANIST: The chief attraction has gone to the john.

*A cry in the back.*

Baal!

MJURK (*drumming on the door*): Sir, don't carry on like that! Hell, I forbid you to shut yourself in. When you're on salary with me. I've got it in writing. You crook! (*Drums frantically.*)

LUPU (*in the door right, where the blue night is visible*): The toilet window is open. The vulture has flown. No brandy, no poetry.

MJURK: Empty? Flown? Gone through the toilet? Swindler! I'll go straight to the police! (*Rushes out.*)

VOICES (*shouting rhythmically, from the back*): Baal! Baal! Baal!

53

*Green fields, blue plum trees.*

BAAL. EKART.

BAAL (*slowly, through the fields*): Ever since, the sky has been greener, and pregnant, air of July, wind, no shirt in one's pants! (*To* EKART *in the back:*) They chafe my bare thighs. My skull's inflated by the wind. The smell of the fields clings to the hair under my armpits. The air's trembling, as if it had got drunk on brandy.

EKART (*behind him*): Why do you run away from the plum trees like an elephant?

BAAL: Place your paw on my skull: it swells with each pulse beat and then collapses again like a bubble. Can't you feel it?

EKART: No.

BAAL: You know nothing of my soul.

EKART: Why don't we go and lie in the water?

BAAL: My soul, brother, is the groaning of the cornfields when they roll in the wind, and the glitter in the eyes of two insects that want to gobble each other up.

EKART: A boy driven mad by July, a boy with immortal viscera, that's you. A dumpling that will one day leave the sky marked with grease stains!

BAAL: Words, words, words. But no matter.

EKART: My body is as light as a small plum in the wind.

BAAL: That's because of the pale sky of summer, brother. Shall we have ourselves soaked in the lukewarm water of a blue pool? Otherwise the white roads will hoist us, like angels' ropes, into the sky.

*Village tavern. Evening.*

FARMERS *around* BAAL. EKART *in a corner.*

BAAL: It's good I have you all together here. My brother
    will be here tomorrow evening. By then the bulls
    must all be here too.

ONE FARMER (*with open mouth*): How can you tell if a
    bull is like your brother wants it?

BAAL: Only my brother can tell that. They must all be
    first rate, that's all, or it's no deal. One corn brandy,
    landlord!

SECOND FARMER: And you'll buy it right away?

BAAL: The one with the strongest loins, yes.

THIRD FARMER: They'll be bringing bulls from eleven vil-
    lages for the money you're putting up.

FIRST FARMER: Take a look at *my* bull!

BAAL: Landlord, a corn brandy!

FARMERS: My bull's the best!—Tomorrow evening, you
    say? (*They make ready to go.*) Are you staying here
    over night?

BAAL: Yes. In a bed.

    FARMERS *exeunt.*

EKART: What are you up to? Have you gone crazy?

BAAL: Wasn't it splendid, how they blinked and stared
    until finally they got it and started counting?

EKART: Well, at least it's earned us a few shots of corn
    brandy. But now we'll have to leave in quite a
    hurry.

BAAL: In a hurry, now? Have you gone crazy?

EKART: You're the crazy one. Just think of those bulls!

BAAL: What do you think I've bamboozled these fellows
    for?

EKART: For a few brandies! ?

BAAL: Nothing of the kind. I want to give you a real treat, Ekart. (*He opens the window behind him. It is getting dark. He sits down again.*)

EKART: Six brandies have made you drunk. You should be ashamed of yourself.

BAAL: It will be magnificent. I love these simple people. I'll provide you with a divine spectacle, brother. Cheers!

EKART: You like to play naive. The poor fellows will smash my head in, and yours!

BAAL: They're doing it for their own edification. On a warm evening like this I think of them with a certain tenderness. They come here to do some swindling in their own simple way, and I like that.

EKART (*getting up*): Well, it's the bulls or me. I'll go, provided the landlord hasn't smelled a rat.

BAAL (*somber*): The evening is so warm. Stay another hour. Then I'll come with you. You know I love you. One can sit here and smell the manure from the fields. Do you think the landlord will sell another brandy to people who play tricks with bulls?

EKART: I can hear footsteps.

PARSON *enters*.

PARSON (*to* BAAL): Good evening. You are the man with the bulls?

BAAL: I am.

PARSON: What have you started this swindle for?

BAAL: We see nothing else on this earth. How strong the smell of hay is from over there! Is it always like this in the evening?

PARSON: Your world seems a very poor one, my man.

BAAL: My sky is full of trees and bodies.

PARSON: Don't talk that way. The world is not your circus.

BAAL: No? Then what is it?

56

PARSON: Now listen, I'm a very good-natured man. I don't intend to be vindictive. I've cleared the matter up.

BAAL: The righteous one has no sense of humor, Ekart.

PARSON: Don't you see how childish your plan was? (*To* EKART:) What does he want?

BAAL (*leans back*): In the dusk, in the evening—of course, it has to be evening and of course the sky must be cloudy—when the air is mild and there's a breeze, the bulls are coming. Trotting in from all points of the compass, a tremendous spectacle. And then the poor people stand among them, and don't know what to do with all the bulls, and they have miscalculated: all they get is a tremendous spectacle. Then too I love people who have miscalculated. And where else could you see so many animals in one place?

PARSON: And to this end you propose to stir up seven villages?

BAAL: What are seven villages against my spectacle?

PARSON: Now I understand. You're a poor unfortunate. And I suppose you have a weakness for bulls?

BAAL: Come, Ekart! He's spoiled the whole thing. Christians no longer love animals.

PARSON (*laughs. Then seriously*): I can't let you get away with that. Just go. Make yourself scarce. I think I'm doing you quite a service, my good man.

BAAL: Come, Ekart! You won't get your treat, brother. (*Exits slowly with* EKART.)

PARSON: Good-bye! Landlord, I'll pay for those gentlemen.

LANDLORD (*behind the table*): Eleven brandies, your reverence.

*Trees. Evening.*

*Six or seven* LUMBERJACKS *sitting about, leaning against trees,* BAAL *among them. In the grass, a corpse.*

FIRST LUMBERJACK: It was an oak. He didn't die all at once. He suffered a while.

SECOND LUMBERJACK: This morning he said the weather seemed to be improving. That's how he wanted it: green with some rain. And the timber not too dry.

THIRD LUMBERJACK: He was a good lad, was Teddy. Before he came here he had a small shop someplace. That was in his heyday. He was as fat as a clergyman then. But he ruined his business for some woman and came up here and lost his paunch as the years went by.

FOURTH LUMBERJACK: Did he never talk about that affair?

THIRD LUMBERJACK: No. I don't know, either, whether he wanted to go back where he came from. He saved a good deal of money, maybe because he had such moderate tastes. Up here we all tell nothing but lies. It's better that way.

FIRST LUMBERJACK: A week ago he said he'd go up north in the winter. It seems he had a cabin up there somewhere. (*To* BAAL:) Didn't he tell you where, Elephant? You spoke to him about it, didn't you?

BAAL: Leave me alone. I know nothing.

THIRD LUMBERJACK: I suppose you want to live in it yourself?

SECOND LUMBERJACK: You can't rely on the fellow. Do you remember how he dropped our boots in the water at night, so we couldn't go to work in the forest, merely because he was lazy, as always?

FOURTH LUMBERJACK: He does nothing to earn his wages.

BAAL: Don't quarrel! Can't you think of poor Teddy for a moment?

FIRST LUMBERJACK: Where were *you* when he got his?

BAAL *gets up and goes across the grass to* TEDDY. *Sits down beside him.*

Baal can't walk straight, boys!

SECOND LUMBERJACK: Leave him alone! The Elephant is moved!

THIRD LUMBERJACK: You really could be a bit quieter with him still lying here.

FOURTH LUMBERJACK: What are you doing with Teddy, Elephant?

BAAL (*over him*): He has his rest; we have our restlessness; both are all right. The sky is black. The trees are trembling. Somewhere clouds are billowing. That's the picture. One can eat. After sleep we wake up; he doesn't; both are all right.

FOURTH LUMBERJACK: What do you say the sky is?

BAAL: The sky is black.

FOURTH LUMBERJACK: You aren't very strong in the head. It always hits the wrong guy.

BAAL: Yes, that is marvelous, my dear man, there you are right.

FIRST LUMBERJACK: It can't hit Baal. He never goes near work.

BAAL: Teddy, on the other hand, was a hard worker. Teddy was generous. Teddy was easy to get on with. And of all this, one thing remains: that Teddy *was*.

SECOND LUMBERJACK: I wonder where he is now?

BAAL (*pointing to the dead man*): There.

THIRD LUMBERJACK: I always think, the spirits of sinners, they're the wind in the evening, in spring particularly, but also in the fall, I think.

BAAL: And in summer, in the sun, above the fields of grain.

THIRD LUMBERJACK: No, that doesn't suit them. It has to be dark.

BAAL: It has to be dark, Teddy.

*Silence.*

FIRST LUMBERJACK: Where are we to put him, boys?

THIRD LUMBERJACK: He has no one who'd want him.

FOURTH LUMBERJACK: He lived for himself alone upon this earth.

SECOND LUMBERJACK: And his things?

THIRD LUMBERJACK: There isn't much. He took his money somewhere. To some bank. It'll stay there if he doesn't claim it. Do you know what, Baal?

BAAL: He doesn't stink yet.

SECOND LUMBERJACK: I've just had a very good idea, boys.

FOURTH LUMBERJACK: Let's have it!

THE MAN WITH THE IDEA: The Elephant isn't the only one with ideas, boys. How about a drink? To Teddy's memory?

BAAL: That would be indecent, Bergmeier.

LUMBERJACKS: Indecent? Nonsense. But what are we to drink? Water? You should be ashamed of yourself, my lad!

THE MAN WITH THE IDEA: Brandy.

BAAL: I vote *for* the motion. Brandy is decent. What brandy?

THE MAN WITH THE IDEA: Teddy's brandy.

LUMBERJACKS: Teddy's?—That's something!—His brandy ration!—Teddy put something by.—Not a bad idea for an idiot, my lad.

THE MAN WITH THE IDEA: A brainstorm, wasn't it? Not bad for you bunkheads! Teddy's brandy for Teddy's funeral! Cheap and at the same time dignified! Has a speech been made in Teddy's honor? Wouldn't that be the appropriate thing?

60

BAAL: I made one.

SEVERAL LUMBERJACKS: When?

BAAL: A while ago. Before you started talking nonsense. It started with: He has his rest, we have our restlessness . . . you always notice things when they are all over.

LUMBERJACKS: Nitwit! Let's get his brandy.

BAAL: It *is* a *shame!*

LUMBERJACKS: Oho. And why, you great big Elephant?

BAAL: It *is* Teddy's property. The little barrel must not be opened. Teddy has a wife and five poor orphan children.

SECOND LUMBERJACK: Four. There are only four.

FOURTH LUMBERJACK: Why do we only hear of this now?

BAAL: Do you propose to rob Teddy's five poor orphan children by drinking their father's brandy? Is that religion?

SECOND LUMBERJACK: Four. Four orphans.

BAAL: Rob Teddy's four orphan children of their brandy.

THIRD LUMBERJACK: Teddy has no family whatever.

BAAL: But those orphans, my dear man, those orphans!

FIRST LUMBERJACK: Oh, you poor dupes of a crazy Elephant! D'you think Teddy's children want to drink Teddy's brandy? All right, it *may* be Teddy's property . . .

BAAL (*interrupting*): It *was* Teddy's property. . . .

FOURTH LUMBERJACK: What's the point of that now?

SECOND LUMBERJACK: It's just hot air. He has no brains.

THIRD LUMBERJACK: It was Teddy's property and so we'll pay for it. With money, good money, boys. Then let the orphans come!

LUMBERJACKS: A good proposition! The Elephant is beaten. He must be crazy not to want any brandy. Let's go and get Teddy's brandy without him!

BAAL (*calling after them*): At least come back here, you damned tomb robbers! (*To* TEDDY:) Poor Teddy! And the trees are quite strong today, and the air is

61

good and soft, and I feel sort of puffed up inside. Poor Teddy, doesn't it amuse you? You are done for, let me tell you; soon you'll stink. And the wind goes on blowing, everything goes on as before, and I know where your cabin is, and your property will be taken by the living, you've left it all in the lurch, I'm afraid, you who wanted nothing but to live in peace. Your body was still pretty good, Teddy, it isn't too bad even now, only slightly damaged on one side, also in the legs. You'd have been through with women. A man can't lay something like that astride a woman. (*He lifts the dead man's leg.*) But all in all, in this body you could have lived with slightly more good will, my boy. Your soul was a damned noble personality but the dwelling was leaky and rats leave a sinking ship. You succumbed to habit, Teddy.

LUMBERJACKS (*returning*): Now look, Elephant! Where's that barrel of brandy from under Teddy's old bed? —Where were you when we were busy with old Teddy? Yes, you! When Teddy wasn't even quite dead? Where were you then, you pig, you grave robber, you protector of Teddy's poor orphan children, huh?

BAAL: There's no proof, my dear boys.

LUMBERJACKS: Where's the brandy, then? In your esteemed opinion, did the barrel itself drink it?— This is a damned serious business, my boy. Get up you! Rise! Walk four paces and then deny that you are shaken, inwardly and outwardly, completely sozzled, you old—! —Get him up, tickle him a bit, boys, this desecrator of Teddy's poor old honor!

BAAL *is stood upright.*

BAAL: You bunch of pigs! At least don't walk on poor Teddy! (*He sits down and puts the corpse's arm in his.*) If you maltreat me, Teddy falls on his face. Is that the respect due to the dead? I'm acting in self-defense. You are seven, se-ven, and sober, and I am one, and drunk. Is it decent, is it honest, seven against one? Calm down! Teddy has calmed down too!

SEVERAL LUMBERJACKS (*sad and indignant*): Nothing is sacred to this fellow!—May God have mercy on his drunken soul!—The most hardboiled of sinners—running around among God's extremities.

BAAL: Sit down, I don't like sanctimoniousness. There must always be some who're brighter and some who're stupider. The latter make up for it by being better workers. You've seen that I work with my brain. (*He starts smoking.*) You never had the right spirit of reverence, my dear fellows. And what do *you* set in motion when you bury good brandy inside you? I achieve new insights, let me tell you. I've said the profoundest things to Teddy! (*He takes some papers out of the latter's breast pocket, which he examines.*) But you had to run off for that miserable brandy. Sit down: look at the sky, growing dark between the trees. Is that nothing? There's no religion in you!

*A cabin.*

*Rain is heard.* BAAL. EKART.

BAAL: Here our white bodies can hibernate in black mud.

EKART: You still haven't brought that meat.

BAAL: I suppose you're still working on your Mass?

EKART: Why think of my Mass? Think of *your* woman! Where have you driven her again in this rain?

BAAL: She runs after us like one demented and hangs round my neck.

EKART: You're sinking lower and lower.

BAAL: I'm too heavy.

EKART: And I suppose you don't count on croaking?

BAAL: I'll fight every inch of the way. I want to go on living even after I lose my skin. I'll withdraw down into my toes. I'll fall on the grass where it's softest, fall like a bull. I'll swallow death and pretend not to notice.

EKART: Since we've been lying here, you've got even fatter.

BAAL (*reaching with his right hand into his left armpit under his shirt*): But my shirt's got looser. The dirtier, the looser. There'd be room for another man in it. But not a fat one. So why are *you* idling your time away, you of the bony body?

EKART: I have a sort of sky inside my skull, very green, and damned high, and my thoughts drift under it like light clouds in the wind. In no special direction. But all this is inside me.

BAAL: You are delirious, alcoholic. Now you see: the past comes home to roost.

EKART: When the D.T.'s are coming on, I notice it in my face.

BAAL: You have a face that leaves a lot of room for wind. Concave. (*Looking at him*:) You have no face. You're nothing at all. You are transparent.

EKART: I'm getting nearer and nearer to a purely mathematical condition.

BAAL: One never knows anything about your life. Why do you never talk about yourself?

EKART: I suppose I have no life. Who's running round outside?

BAAL: You have good ears. There's something you're covering up. You are a wicked man like me. A devil. But one day you'll see rats. Then you'll be a good man again.

SOPHIE BARGER *appears in the door.*

EKART: Is it you, Sophie?

SOPHIE: May I come in now, Baal?

## SCENE 12

*The plains. Sky. Evening.*

BAAL. EKART. SOPHIE.

SOPHIE: My knees are giving way. Why do you run around like you were out of your mind?

BAAL: Because you're a millstone round my neck.

EKART: How can you treat her like that when she's pregnant by you?

SOPHIE: I wanted it myself, Ekart.

BAAL: She wanted it herself. And now she's a millstone round my neck.

EKART: You are bestial. Sit down, Sophie.

SOPHIE (*sits down heavily*): Let him go!

EKART: If you throw her in the gutter, I'll stay with her.

BAAL: She wouldn't stay with *you,* but you would abandon *me* for her sake. It's just like you.

EKART: Twice you've thrown me out of your bed. My girls were a matter of indifference to you but you stole them from me, even though I loved them.

BAAL: Just *because* you loved them. Twice I've desecrated corpses to keep you pure. I need it, I took no pleasure in it, by God!

EKART (*to* SOPHIE): And you still love this blatant beast?

SOPHIE: I can't help it, Ekart. I'd love even his corpse. I love even his fists. I can't help it, Ekart.

BAAL: I don't want to know what you two did while I was in the clink.

SOPHIE: We stood together in front of the white prison.

BAAL: Together.

SOPHIE: Beat me for it.

66

EKART (*yelling*): Didn't you throw her at me?

BAAL: At that time I didn't yet care for you.

EKART: I haven't got your elephant's hide.

BAAL: I love you for that.

EKART: At least keep your damned mouth shut about it while she's around.

BAAL: She should go. She's getting to be a pest. (*Puts both his hands to his throat.*) She washes her dirty linen in your tears. Haven't you noticed yet that she runs naked between the two of us? I'm as patient as a lamb but I can't get out of my own skin.

EKART (*sits down with* SOPHIE): Go home to your mother!

SOPHIE: But I can't!

BAAL: She can't, Ekart.

SOPHIE: Beat me, if you want to, Baal. I won't ask you to slow down again. I didn't mean it. Let me run with you as long as I have feet to run with. Then I'll lie down in the bushes and you needn't look. Don't chase me away, Baal.

BAAL: Lay it in the river, your flabby body. You wanted me to vomit you out.

SOPHIE: Do you want me to lie down right here? You don't want me to lie down right here. You don't know it yet, Baal. You're like a child, you don't mean what you say.

BAAL: I'm fed to the teeth.

SOPHIE: But not tonight, not tonight, Baal. I am afraid, alone. I am afraid of the dark. That's what I'm afraid of.

BAAL: In your condition nobody'll do you any harm.

SOPHIE: But the night. Won't you stay with me, just tonight?

BAAL: To the boatmen. It's midsummernight. They'll be drunk.

SOPHIE: A quarter of an hour.

BAAL: Come, Ekart!

SOPHIE: Where am I to go?

BAAL: To heaven, my beloved!

SOPHIE: With my child?

BAAL: Bury it!

SOPHIE: I only hope you won't live to think of what you're telling me now beneath the beautiful sky you like so much. That's what I'm praying for. On my knees.

EKART: I'll stay with you. And then I'll take you to your mother. If only you'll say you no longer love this animal.

BAAL: She loves me.

SOPHIE: I love this animal.

EKART: Are you still here, animal? Have you no knees? Are you drowned in brandy or in poetry? Degenerate beast! Degenerate beast!

BAAL: Half-wit!

EKART *jumps at him, they wrestle.*

SOPHIE: Jesus Christ! They're wild beasts!

EKART (*while wrestling*): Do you hear what she says: in the undergrowth, and right now, it's getting dark? Degenerate beast! Degenerate beast!

BAAL (*against him, presses* EKART *to his breast*): Now you're at my breast. Can you smell me? I'm holding you: there's more to that than being close to a woman. (*Stops.*) Now you can see the stars above the bushes, Ekart.

EKART (*staring at* BAAL *who is looking at the sky*): I can't master it.

BAAL (*his arm around him*): It's getting dark. We must camp out for the night. There are hollows in the wood where no wind penetrates. Come, I'll tell you stories about the animals. (*He drags him away.*)

SOPHIE (*alone in the dark, shouting*): Baal!

*Wooden brown room in an inn. Night. Wind.*

*At tables* GOOGOO, BOLLEBOLL. *The* BEGGAR *and* MAJA, *the beggarwoman, with her* CHILD *in a box.*

BOLLEBOLL (*playing cards with* GOOGOO): I have no money left. Let's play for our souls.

BEGGAR: Brother Wind wants to come in. But we don't know our cold Brother Wind. Hehehe!

*The* CHILD *cries.*

MAJA: Listen! Something going round the house. I hope it's not some big animal.

BOLLEBOLL: Why, are you horny again?

*A knock at the gate.*

MAJA: Listen! I won't open!

BEGGAR: You'll open.

MAJA: No. No. No. Dear Mother of God, No!

BEGGAR: Bouque la Madonne! Open!

MAJA *crawls to the door.*

MAJA: Who's outside?

*The* CHILD *cries.* MAJA *opens the door.*

BAAL *enters with* EKART.

BAAL: Is this the hospital tavern?

MAJA: Yes, but there are no beds free. (*More impertinent.*) And I'm sick.

BAAL: We've got some champagne.

EKART *has gone to the stove.*

BOLLEBOLL: Come here! Anyone who knows what champagne is fits in here.

BEGGAR: Today there's nothing but classy people here, my dear Parsifal.

BAAL (*goes to the table, takes two bottles from his pockets*): Hm?

BEGGAR: I see ghosts!

BOLLEBOLL: I know where you got the champagne from but I won't give you away.

BAAL: Come, Ekart! Are there any glasses?

MAJA: Cups, my lord, cups! (*She brings some.*)

GOOGOO: I need a cup of my own.

BAAL (*suspiciously*): Are you allowed to drink champagne?

GOOGOO: Please!

BAAL *fills his cup.*

BAAL: What are you suffering from?

GOOGOO: Pleurisy. It's nothing. A slight catarrh. Nothing much.

BAAL (*to* BOLLEBOLL): And you?

BOLLEBOLL: Stomach ulcers. Quite harmless.

BAAL (*to the* BEGGAR): I hope you're suffering from some malady too?

BEGGAR: I am insane.

BAAL· Cheers!—We know each other. *I* am healthy.

BEGGAR: I knew a man who thought he was well. *Thought.* He'd been born and bred in a forest, and one day he went back there, he had to think something over. He found the forest grown very strange, extremely unfamiliar. For many days he walked, deep into the wilderness, for he wanted to find out to what degree he'd become dependent, and how much there was in him still that might help him bear it. There wasn't much. (*Drinks.*)

70

BAAL (*disturbed*): Such a wind! And we'll have to go on tonight, Ekart.

BEGGAR: Yes, the wind. One evening, at dusk, when he was no longer so alone, he walked through the great stillness among the trees and stood under one of them that was very big. (*Drinks.*)

BOLLEBOLL: It was the monkey in him.

BEGGAR: Yes, maybe it was the monkey. He leaned against it, very close, felt the life inside it or thought he felt it, and said: you are higher than I, and you stand firm, and you know the earth below, and it holds you up. I can run and move better, but I don't stand firm and cannot go below and nothing holds me up. Also the great stillness above the treetops in the infinite sky is unknown to me. (*Drinks.*)

GOOGOO: What did the tree say?

BEGGAR: Yes. The wind blew. A tremor ran through the tree. The man felt it. So he threw himself down, embraced the wild, hard roots, and wept bitter tears. But he did that with many trees.

EKART: Did he get better?

BEGGAR: No. But he died more easily.

MAJA: I don't understand.

BEGGAR: No one understands anything. But you can feel some things. Tales that can be understood are just badly told.

BOLLEBOLL: Do you believe in God?

BAAL (*with difficulty*): I always believed in myself. But one *could* become an atheist.

BOLLEBOLL (*laughs loudly*): Now I'm getting gay! God! Champagne! Love! Wind and rain! (*Tries to grasp* MAJA.)

MAJA: Leave me alone. A smell comes out of your mouth.

BOLLEBOLL: And have *you* not got syphilis? (*Sits her in his lap.*)

BEGGAR: Beware! (*To* BOLLEBOLL:) I'm getting drunk.

71

And you can't go out into the rain tonight if I'm dead drunk.

GOOGOO (*to* EKART): He was handsomer, that's why he got her.

EKART: And your intellectual superiority? Your spiritual preponderance?

GOOGOO: She wasn't like that. She was *completely* unspoilt.

EKART: And what did you do?

GOOGOO: I felt ashamed.

BOLLEBOLL: Listen! The wind! He is begging God for peace.

MAJA (*sings*):

Eiapopeia, the wind's on the moors
While we are warm and drunk indoors.

BAAL: What child is this?

MAJA: My daughter, your lordship.

BEGGAR: A *virgo dolorosa!*

BAAL (*drinks*): That's past now, Ekart. Yes. That, too, was beautiful.

EKART: What?

BOLLEBOLL: He's forgotten that.

BAAL: The pa-a-ast, what a strange word!

GOOGOO (*to* EKART): The most beautiful thing is: Nothing.

BOLLEBOLL: Hush! Now comes Googoo's aria! The bag of worms sings!

GOOGOO· It is like the trembling air on summer evenings. The sun. But it does not tremble. Nothing. Nothing whatever. One simply ceases. The wind blows, but one is no longer cold. It rains, one is no longer wet. Jokes happen, one does not laugh. One's body rots, one does not have to wait. General Strike.

BEGGAR: This is the paradise of hell.

GOOGOO: Yes, it is paradise. No wish remains unfulfilled. There is no wish left. You are cured of all bad habits. Even wishes. So you are free.

72

MAJA: And what happens in the end?
GOOGOO: Nothing. Nothing whatever. There is no end.
Nothing lasts forever.
BOLLEBOLL: Amen.
BAAL (*has got up. To* EKART): Ekart, get up! We've
fallen among murderers. (*Holds* EKART *around the
shoulders.*) The worms inflate themselves. Putrefac-
tion crawls toward us. The worms sing each other's
praises.
EKART: It's the second time you've done this. I wonder
if it comes from drinking alone?
BAAL: My intestines are on display. . . . This is no
mudbath.
EKART: Sit down! Fill yourself with drink! Warm yourself!
MAJA (*sings, somewhat drunk*):

Summer and winter, rain and snow,
When you're drunk you feel no woe.

BOLLEBOLL (*has embraced* MAJA, *struggles with her*):
That aria always tickles me pink, little Googoo.
. . . My little itsibitsy Maja.

*The* CHILD *cries.*

BAAL (*drinks*): Who are you? (*Irritatedly to* GOOGOO:)
Bag of worms they call you. Are you on the danger
list? Cheers! (*Sits down.*)
BEGGAR: Beware, Bolleboll! Champagne doesn't agree
with me.
MAJA (*leaning against* BOLLEBOLL, *sings*):

Close your eyes now, looking makes them sore,
Come, let's sleep, so you'll feel it no more.

BAAL (*sings, with brutality*):

Swim down the river with rats in your hair:
The sky will still be marvelous up there.

*(Gets up, the glass in his hand.)* Black is the sky. What startled you? *(Drums on the table.)* You have to be able to stand the merry-go-round. It is wonderful. *(Staggers.)* I want to be an elephant in the circus and make water when everything isn't just right. *(Starts to dance, sings.)* Dance with the wind, poor corpse, sleep with the cloud, you decadent God! *(He staggers to the table.)*

EKART *(drunk, has got up)*: Now I won't go with you any more. I too have a soul. You've spoiled my soul. You spoil everything. And now, too, I'll start work on my Mass.

BAAL: I love you, cheers!

EKART· But I won't go with you. *(Sits down.)*

BEGGAR *(to BOLLEBOLL)*: Take your hands off her, you pig.

MAJA: Mind your own business.

BEGGAR: Hold your tongue, miserable creature!

MAJA: You madman, you're raving!

BOLLEBOLL *(poisonously)*: A swindle! He's not sick. That's it. It's all a swindle!

BEGGAR: And you've got cancer!

BOLLEBOLL *(with uncanny calm)*: I've got cancer?

BEGGAR *(cowardly)*: I didn't say anything. Leave her alone!

MAJA *laughs.*

BAAL: Why does it cry? *(Moves across to the box.)*

BEGGAR *(angrily)*: What do you want with the baby?

BAAL *(bends over the box)*: Why do you cry? Haven't you seen it all before? Or do you cry each time afresh?

BEGGAR: Leave it alone, man. *(Throws his glass at BAAL.)*

MAJA *(jumps up)*: You pig!

BOLLEBOLL: He only wants a peep under her skirt.

BAAL *(slowly gets up)*: Oh, you pigs! You don't know humanity! *(Broadly, by the table, very loud, with*

74

*simplicity*.) Seven years ago I slept with my boss's wife. She was full and wild. I'd forgotten her face in all this time, but now I know it again and what it was like. It was a bright day. She had a child and then she caught hell for it at home. I've not seen her since, I don't know what became of her. That's life. Come, Ekart, we'll wash ourselves clean in the river! (*Exits with* EKART.)

## SCENE 14

*Green thicket of leaves. A river behind it.* BAAL.

BAAL (*sitting among the leaves*): The water is warm. We can lie on the sand like lobsters. And the green bushes and the white clouds in the sky. Ekart!

EKART (*hidden*): What is it?

BAAL: I love you.

EKART: I'm too comfortable, lying here.

BAAL: Did you see the clouds just now?

EKART: Yes. They have no shame.

*Silence.*

A moment ago a woman went by.

BAAL: I have no further need of women. . . .

*Highway. Willows.*

*Wind. Night.* EKART *asleep in the grass.*

BAAL (*coming across the fields, as if drunk, his clothes open, like a sleepwalker*): Ekart! Ekart! I've got it. Wake up!

EKART: Got what? Are you talking in your sleep again?

BAAL (*sits down beside him*): This:

> And when she was drowned and floated down
> From rivulets and into larger rivers
> The azure heavens glowed most marvelously
> As though they must propitiate the body.
>
> Seaweed and algae, both held on to her,
> And she slowly grew much heavier.
> Coolly fishes brushed against her leg.
> Animals and plants weighed down the voyage.
>
> And the evening sky grew dark as smoke
> And held, when evening passed, the light suspended.
> In the morning brightness came again.
> There was night and morning even for her.
>
> When her pale corpse rotted in the water
> It befell that slowly God forgot her:
> First her face; her hands then; then her hair.
> In carrion-carrying rivers she was carrion.

*Wind.*

EKART: Is it haunting you already, the ghost? It isn't as

evil as you. Only, one's sleep has gone to the devil, and the wind is playing the organ again in the willow stumps. So again there remains only the white breast of philosophy, darkness, wetness, to our blessed end; and even among old women, only second sight.

BAAL: In this wind you don't need brandy, you're drunk already. I see the world in a mellow light: it is the Lord God's excrement.

EKART: The Lord God, who sufficiently declared his true nature once and for all in combining the sexual organ with the urinary tract!

BAAL (*lying on the ground*): It is all so beautiful.

*Wind.*

EKART: The willows are like rotten stumps of teeth in the black mouth of the sky.—I'll be starting on my Mass soon.

BAAL: Finished your quartet?

EKART: Where would I find the time?

*Wind.*

BAAL: There's a redhead, a pale one. You maul her, don't you?

EKART: She has a soft white body and comes to the willows at noon. The willows have branches that hang down like hair. We fuck in there like squirrels.

BAAL: Is she better-looking than me?

*Darkness. The wind continues to play the organ.*

*Young hazel bushes \* with long red stalks hanging down.*
BAAL *sitting inside them. Noon.*

BAAL: I'll simply satisfy her, the white pigeon. . . .
    (*Looking the place over.*) From here the clouds
    look beautiful through the willow branches. When
    he comes, he'll only see skin. I'm fed up with these
    love affairs of his. Be still, my soul!

*A* YOUNG WOMAN *enters from the thicket, red hair,
full, pale.*

    (*Without looking round:*) Is it *you*?
YOUNG WOMAN: Where's your friend?
BAAL: Composing a Mass in E-flat minor.
YOUNG WOMAN: Tell him I came.
BAAL: He's getting so thin you can almost see through
    him. He practices self-abuse. He's falling back into
    zoology. Do sit down. (*He looks round.*)

YOUNG WOMAN: I'd rather stand.
BAAL (*draws himself up on the willow branches*): He's
    been eating too many eggs lately.
YOUNG WOMAN: I love him.
BAAL: What do I care? (*Grabs her.*)
YOUNG WOMAN: Don't touch me! You're too dirty!
BAAL (*slowly touching her throat*): That's your throat?
    Do you know how pigeons are finished off? Or wild
    ducks in the undergrowth?
YOUNG WOMAN: Jesus Christ! (*Tears at him.*) Leave me
    alone!

---

\* "Willows" in the dialogue, however. (E. B., M. E.)

BAAL: With your weak knees? You are falling over. You want to be layed among the willows? A man's a man: in that respect most of them are alike. (*Takes her in his arms.*)

YOUNG WOMAN (*trembling*): Please let me go! Please!

BAAL: A shameless quail. Come on then. Desperate man performs heroic rescue! (*Takes her by both arms and drags her into the bushes.*)

*Maple in the wind.*

*Cloudy sky.* BAAL *and* EKART *sitting among the roots.*

BAAL: Drinking's a necessity, Ekart, have you any money left?

EKART: No. Look at the maple tree in the wind!

BAAL: It's trembling.

EKART: Where's the girl you've been dragging round the taverns?

BAAL: Turn into a fish and look for her.

EKART: You are overfeeding, Baal, you'll burst.

BAAL: An explosion I'd love to hear!

EKART: Don't you sometimes look into the water when it's black and deep and no fish in it yet? Beware of falling in! You have to be careful. You're so very heavy, Baal.

BAAL: It's a *person* I must beware of. I've made a song. Want to hear it?

EKART: Read it and I'll know you.

BAAL: It's called "Death in the Forest."

In the forest eternal a man lies dead,
Streams in flood below, winds screaming overhead.
He died like a beast. He clung to the roots of a tree
And he stared at the lofty top of tree on tree.
The storm raged on.

And those who round about him sat
Stood up and said: "Be calm. This is the end.
So let us take you homewards, friend."

But he fought back with his knees and spat
And asked those men: "Home, where is that?"
Nor child nor land had he.

"That mouth! Just look at the rotten teeth!
Will you go naked on the eternal heath?
Rotten your clothes, your bone, your brain,
Dead your old nag and empty your purse?
Die calmly! You've gone from bad to worse.
Why would you want to be hungry again?"

Round him, round them, how the forest did roar!
They heard him cry to the darkling sky
And they could see how he clutched that tree
And a shudder ran through them as never before.
They trembled and clenched their fingers in a ball.
For he was a man like them all.

"You no-good beast! You're mangy, you're nuts!
A bum! A heap of pus and guts!
With your greedy gasping you grab our air,
                                              lunkhead!"
And he, the suppurating wound, he said:
"I want to live and let the sunlight through.
I want to ride in the light like you."

It was a thing no friend could understand.
They trembled. They were speechless with disgust.
And the earth, it took him by his naked hand.
From sea to sea stretches the windswept land.
"Must I lie down and be calm? I must."

Such was his poor life's overplus
That in the morning twilight, he
Pressed his own carrion in the murky grass
And died. All hatred and disgust
They buried him under branches of the tree.

And out of the thicket, and out of the night,

They rode till, turning, they could espy
That tree-grave towering toward the sky.
And all of them wondered at the sight
For the top of the tree was full of light.
They crossed their young faces and rode on
Into the heath and into the sun.

EKART: Yes. Yes. It seems we've come to this.

BAAL: When I can't sleep at night, I look at the stars.
That's just like the other thing.

EKART: Is it?

BAAL (*suspiciously*): But I don't do that often. It
weakens you.

EKART (*after a while*): You've been writing a good deal
of poetry lately. Not had a woman in a long time,
I suppose.

BAAL: How so?

EKART: Can you deny it?

BAAL *gets up, stretches himself, looks up to the top
of the maple tree, laughs.*

SCENE 18

*Bar room.*

*Evening. The* WAITRESS. WATZMANN. JOHANNES, *ragged, in shabby overcoat with upturned collar, hopelessly gone to seed. The* WAITRESS *has Sophie's features.*

EKART: It's eight years now.

*They drink. Wind blows.*

JOHANNES: At twenty-five life should be just beginning. They get broader and bear children.

*Silence.*

WATZMANN: His mother died yesterday. He's running round borrowing money for the funeral. He'll be coming here with it. We'll be able to pay for our brandy then. The landlord's decent: gives credit on a corpse that was once a mother. (*Drinks.*)

JOHANNES: Baal! The wind no longer fills his sails!

WATZMANN (*to* EKART): I suppose you have to put up with a lot?

EKART: One can't spit in his face: he is sinking.

WATZMANN (*to* JOHANNES): Does that hurt? Does it worry you?

JOHANNES: It's a pity, his going to waste, I tell you. (*Drinks.*)

*Silence.*

WATZMANN: He's getting more and more disgusting.

EKART· Don't say that. I don't want to hear it. I love him I never hold anything against him. Because I love him. He's a child.

84

WATZMANN: He only does what he must do. Because he's so lazy.

EKART (*stands in the door*): It is a very mild night. The wind's warm. Like milk. I love all that. One should never drink. Or not so much. (*Back to the table.*) The night is very mild. Now and for another three weeks into the fall one can live quite well on the road. (*Sits down.*)

WATZMANN: Are you leaving tonight? I suppose you want to get rid of him? You're sick of him?

JOHANNES: Take care.

BAAL *slowly comes into the doorway.*

WATZMANN: Is that you, Baal?

EKART (*hard*): What do you want this time?

BAAL (*enters, sits down*): What a miserable hole this has turned into!

*The* WAITRESS *brings brandy.*

WATZMANN: Nothing's changed here. Only you, it seems, have grown more refined.

BAAL: Is that still *you*, Louise?

*Silence.*

JOHANNES: Yes, it's cosy here.—I mean, I *have* to drink, to drink a lot. It makes you strong. Admittedly, even then one's road to hell is paved with open jack-knives. But it's different, nevertheless. As though one's knees were buckling, you know: yielding. So that one doesn't feel them, the knives. Elastic knees. Besides, in the past I never had such funny ideas. Never had such ideas when I lived in respectable circumstances. Only now I have ideas. I've become a genius. Hm.

EKART (*erupts*): I'd like to be in the fields again in the morning. Between the tree trunks the light is lemon-colored. I want to go up again into the forests.

JOHANNES: I can't understand that. Baal, you must pay for another round of brandy. It's really cosy here.

BAAL: Another brandy for . . .

JOHANNES: No names! We know each other. You know, at night I sometimes dream such dreadful things. But only sometimes. It's extremely cosy now.

*The wind blows. They drink.*

WATZMANN (*hums*):

There were still splendid trees by the thousand
Inviting, shady, high.
You can hang yourself from a treetop
Or beneath a tree you can lie.*

BAAL: When was everything like this before? It was exactly like this once.

JOHANNES: I mean: she's *still* floating. Nobody ever found her. Only I sometimes have the feeling, you know, that she is floating down my throat in all that brandy, a tiny little corpse, half rotten. And yet she was seventeen. Now she's got rats and seaweed in her green hair, it suits her quite well . . . a little puffed up, a little white, filled with stinking river mud, quite black. She used to be so clean. That's why she went into the river and got to be smelly.

---

* Watzmann is singing a song of which the full text is given in the *Hauspostille*. I translate as follows:

*Orge's Answer When a Rope and Soap Were Offered Him*

If my life should improve, remarked Orge,
That would certainly suit me.
For his life was quite bad, added Orge,
Yet his life was better than he.

Rope and soap he would take them both gladly:
It's a shame, he'd have you know,
That by living on this planet he'd got
Filthy from top to toe.

86

WATZMANN: What is flesh? It rots like spirit. Gentle-men, I am dead drunk. Twice two is four. So I'm *not* drunk. But I have intimations of a higher world. Bow down, be hu-humble! Cast the old Adam off. (*Drinks, trembling and intense.*) I'm not quite done for yet, as long as I have my intimations and I can still figure quite nicely that twice two . . . What a funny word: twice! Twi-ice! (*Sits down.*)

BAAL (*takes the guitar and smashes the light with it*): Now I'll sing. (*Sings.*)

Scorched by the sun, eroded by the rainstorms,
His stolen laurels in his tousled hair
He forgot his childhood except for childhood's
daydreams
Forgot the roof, remembered the sky above.

My voice is clear as a bell. (*Tunes the guitar.*)

---

And yet there were mountains and valleys
More indeed than one ever knew.
One got more from the whole thing the choosier
One showed onself passing through.

And so long as the sun was still up there
So long it was not too late.
And he'd wait just as long as it stayed there
And as long as it took to set.

There were still splendid trees by the thousand
Inviting, shady, high.
You can hang yourself from a treetop
Or beneath a tree you can lie.

And as for one's last bit of real
Estate one holds on to it.
And one holds on with tooth and with nail to
Even one's last bit of shit.

And yet only when hate and disgust shall
Reach up to his throat shall he
Cut that throat without any grimacing
And most likely nonchalantly.

(E.B.)

87

EKART: Sing on, Baal!
BAAL (*goes on singing*):

> You who were banished out of hell and heaven
> You murderers to whom much woe befell
> Why did you not stay inside the wombs of your
> mothers
> Where it was calm, and one slumbered, and one
> was?

The guitar is out of tune.

WATZMANN: Good song. Fits me exactly. Romanticism!
BAAL (*sings*):

> But he is seeking still in seas of absinth
> Although his mother has forgot him now
> Grinning and cursing and from time to time weeping
> The country where there is a better life.

WATZMANN: Now I can't find my glass. The table's shaking like mad. Put the light on. How's one to find one's mouth? !
EKART: Nonsense. Can you see, Baal?
BAAL: I don't want to. It's nice in the dark. With champagne inside you, and nostalgia without memory. Are you my friend, Ekart?
EKART (*with difficulty*): Yes, but go on singing!
BAAL (*sings*):

> Dancing through hells and whipped through
> paradises
> And drunk on showers of unheard-of light
> He dreams at times about a little meadow
> With some blue sky above it and that is all.

JOHANNES: Now I'll stay with you forever. You can take me along quite easily. I hardly eat anything nowadays.

WATZMANN (*has put some light on with great difficulty*):
Let there be light! Hehehehe!

BAAL: It hurts one's eyes. (*Gets up.*)

EKART (*the* WAITRESS *on his lap, laboriously gets up and tries to free his neck of her arm*): What's the matter with you? It's nothing. Ridiculous.

BAAL *crouches to jump at him.*

You won't be jealous of her?

BAAL *feels his way forward, a cup falls.*

Why shouldn't I have women?

BAAL *looks at him.*

Am I your lover?

BAAL *throws himself at him, chokes him. The light goes out.* WATZMANN *laughs drunkenly, the* WAITRESS *screams. Other guests from the room next door enter with a lamp.*

WATZMANN: He has a knife.

WAITRESS: He's murdering him. Jesus!

THE MEN (*throw themselves on the wrestling bodies*):
For the devil's sake, man. Let him go! The fellow has stabbed him! God almighty!

BAAL *gets up.*

*Dusk falls suddenly. The lamp goes out.*

BAAL: Ekart!

*Ten degrees latitude east of Greenwich.*

*Forest.* BAAL *with his guitar, his hands in his pockets, going off.*

BAAL: The pale wind in the black trees. Trees like Lupu's wet hair. At about eleven the moon rises. Then it's light enough. This is a small forest. I'll go down into the big ones. I've been running on thick soles ever since I've been alone again in my skin. I must keep on bearing north. Follow the underside of the leaves. I must leave that little affair behind me. Forward! (*Sings.*)

Baal, he blinks at well-fed vultures overhead
Waiting up among the stars till Baal is dead.

    *Going off.*

Often Baal shams dead. So if the bird
Falls for this, Baal dines on vulture, without a word.

*A gust of wind.*

*Highway. Evening. Wind. Squalls of rain.*
*Two* RANGERS *fighting the wind.*

FIRST RANGER: The black rain and this Allhallows wind!
    This damn bum!
SECOND RANGER: It seems he's heading north, toward the
    forests. Up there no one will ever find him.
FIRST RANGER: What's the matter with him?
SECOND RANGER: Above all: he's a murderer. Earlier:
    vaudeville artist and poet. Then he owned a merry-
    go-round, was a lumberjack, a millionairess's lover,
    a convict and a pimp. After the murder they caught
    him, but he's strong as an elephant. All on account
    of a waitress, a registered prostitute. On her account
    he stabbed his best friend.
FIRST RANGER: A man like that has no soul. He belongs
    to the animal kingdom.
SECOND RANGER: And with all that, he's like a child.
    Carries logs for old ladies so he almost gets caught.
    Never owned anything. The waitress was the end.
    And for her he killed his best friend, also a some-
    what doubtful character.
FIRST RANGER: If only we could find some brandy some-
    place. Or a woman. Let's go. This place gives me
    the creeps. There's something moving over there.

*Exeunt both.*

BAAL, *out of the bushes, with his pack and guitar.*
*Whistles through his teeth.*
BAAL: So he's dead? Poor little animal! Getting in my
    way like that! It's beginning to be interesting. (*Fol-
    lows the two* RANGERS.)

*Wind.*

*Log cabin in a forest.*

*Night. Wind.* BAAL *on a dirty bed.* MEN *playing cards and drinking.*

FIRST MAN (*by* BAAL's *bed*): What do you want? You're on your last legs. Any child can see that. Who's interested in you? Have you got anyone? There you are, there you are. Bring your teeth together if you have anyone left. Sometimes a guy bites the dust who might still get a lot of fun out of life, a millionaire. But you—you haven't even got identification papers. Don't be afraid: round as a ball, the world will roll on. Tomorrow morning the wind will be whistling. Try to be more detached. Say to yourself: "A rat is dying. So what?" Just take it easy. You haven't any teeth left.

MEN· Is it still pouring? We'll have to spend the night with the corpse.—Shut up! Trumps!—Still got breath in you, fatty? Go on, sing: "In the white womb of his mother . . ." —Leave him: he'll be cold before the black rain stops. Go on with the game. —He drank like a bottomless pit, but there's something in that pallid hunk that makes you think of yourself. Ten of spades! Concentrate, boys, it's not a game, if you don't take it seriously, we won't get a decent game out of it.

*Silence, only occasional curses.*

BAAL: What time is it?
FIRST MAN: Eleven. You leaving?

BAAL: Soon. The road's bad?

FIRST MAN: Rain.

MEN (*getting up*): Now the rain's stopped. It's time—
everything will be dripping wet—that fellow's allowed to be idle again. (*They take their axes.*)

FIRST MAN (*stepping in front of* BAAL, *spitting on the
floor*): Good night and so long. Are you going to
croak?

SECOND MAN: Going to bite the dust? Incognito?

THIRD MAN: You better watch how you start stinking
tomorrow. We'll be out felling trees till noon, and
then we'll be wanting to eat.

BAAL: Couldn't you stay here a while?

MEN (*with much laughter*): Want us to play mammy?
—Want to sing your swan song? Want to confess,
you brandy bottle?—Can't you vomit by yourself?

BAAL: If you could only stay thirty minutes.

MEN (*with much laughter*): You know what: drop dead
by yourself!—Come on, the wind's fallen.—What
about you?

FIRST MAN: I'll follow.

BAAL: It won't take long now, gentlemen.

*Laughter.*

You, too, will dislike dying alone, gentlemen.

*Laughter.*

THIRD MAN: Old woman! Here's something to remember
me by. (*Spits in his face.*)

*All move toward the door.*

BAAL: Twenty minutes.

*The* MEN *exeunt through the open door.*

FIRST MAN (*in the door*): Stars.

BAAL: Wipe the spittle off.

FIRST MAN: Where?

BAAL: My forehead.

FIRST MAN: There. Why do you laugh?

BAAL: I like the taste.

FIRST MAN (*indignant*): You're through. Good-bye. (*With his axe, to the door.*)

BAAL: Thank you.

FIRST MAN: Is there anything I could still . . . no, I must get to work. Christ! Corpses!

BAAL: You! Come closer!

*FIRST MAN bends over him.*

One could make quite good use of . . .

FIRST MAN: Of what?

BAAL: Everything.

FIRST MAN: You old gormandizer. (*Laughs aloud, exits.*)

*The door stays open, one sees a blue night.*

BAAL (*worried*): You! Fellow!

FIRST MAN (*through the window*): Huh?

BAAL: Are you going?

FIRST MAN: To work.

BAAL: Where?

FIRST MAN: What does it matter to you?

BAAL: What's the time?

FIRST MAN: Quarter past eleven. (*Exits.*)

BAAL: He's gone to the devil.

*Silence.*

One two three four five six. It doesn't help.

*Silence.*

Mother! Ekart should go away! The sky's so damned near, you can touch it. Everything's dripping wet again. Sleep. One. Two. Three. Four. It's so stuffy in here. Out there it must be light. I want to go

94

outside. (*Lifts himself.*) I'll go out. My dear Baal. (*Sharply.*) I'm not a rat. It must be lighter out there. My dear Baal. You'll get to the door. You still have knees, it's better in the doorway. Damn! My dear Baal. (*He crawls on all fours to the threshold.*) Stars . . . hm. (*He crawls out.*)

*The End*

These tunes appear, with no composer's name, in the 1927 edition of *Die Hauspostille*.

**1.** Chorale of the Great Baal

**2.** Orge's Hymn

### 3. Orge's Answer

"If my life shall im - prove," re-marked Or - ge, "That will cer-tain-ly suit me" For his life was quite bad, add-ed Or - ge, yet his life was bet - ter than he.

### 4. Ballad of the Adventurers

Scorched by the sun er-od-ed by the rain-storms His stol-en lau - rels in his tousl - ed hair he for-got his child-hood ex-cept for child-hood's day - dreams For-got the roof re-mem-bered the sky a - bove.

# A Man's A Man

# ACKNOWLEDGMENTS

I have had expert help and advice in the rendering of this Brecht play from Dr. Hugo Schmidt and Mr. Martin Esslin.

As far as production is concerned, I owe a heavy debt of gratitude to all who have made two productions a success—producers, actors, designers, those of the Loeb Drama Center, Cambridge, Massachusetts, and those of the Masque Theatre, New York City. Road blocks were thrown in the path of both productions, and we had to travel in tanks to drive through them. My New York producers, Mr. and Mrs. Konrad Matthaei, proved especially intrepid tank drivers. I hereby award them medals for services above and beyond the call of duty.

A word of thanks is also due to Mr. Clair Roskam of Camera Three and his associates with CBS-TV who placed part of our show before their viewers at a critical time. One of these associates, Mr. Anthony Wolff, has supplied the admirable photographs of the present volume.

My lyrics were set to music by Joseph Raposo: it would be hard to estimate how much both shows owe to the music alone.

I dedicate this adaptation to the young director of both productions. Neither production would have taken place were it not for his faith and tenacity.

— E.B.

# INTRODUCTION

## Brecht and the Rule of Force

There is Brecht the fad, and there is Brecht the living presence. What manner of man, of artist, is the Brecht who is a living presence in America today?

Not a communist. Nor is American youth afraid of communism, as their seniors were ten years ago. They take it coolly. In talking to students, I notice how much more excited I am likely to get on this subject than they are. It shocks them not at all that Brecht was a sympathizer with communism, though few of them sympathize with it themselves.

A group of them are what some time ago we would have called Fellow Travelers. It would be more accurate to call them *fidelistas,* for Castro is their hero, not Mao nor Krushchev, let alone the late Josef Stalin. And Bertolt Brecht is their hero, too, if they are at all interested in theatre, poetry, or drama. If there is to be an American cult of Brecht with more life to it than we find among the Brechtians of the New York theatre world, then it would be from the young of the New Left that it would come.

The New Left in America has this in common with the old left in America: it gives an impression of far greater strength than it really possesses. To hear people talk now, you'd think we who were in college in the thirties were either Red or lived surrounded by Reds. We weren't. We didn't. May there be no myth in the future to the effect that the students of 1962 were "New Leftists!" If one must generalize, and if one must pretend that the largest homogeneous minority is really a majority, then 1962 is the time, not of Leftism and Castro, but of Pacifism and Erich Fromm and Norman Thomas and H. Stuart Hughes. And this is extremely interesting in relation to Bertolt Brecht, since war had provided the experience which determined his outlook, and opposition to war was his most consistently held stance. True, in 1928 he was converted to Marxism, and he stuck by the policies of Stalin until death came in 1956—except possibly in the privacy of a journal which has not yet been published. Even so, there were ambiguities in Brecht's communism, as the Communists were perhaps the first to point out. If communism was the solution, it was a desperate solution, accepted in the spirit of Pascal's wager. In his last years Brecht is said to have called the West an old whore and the East a young one—preferable only because she was pregnant. Now, Brecht called on no such cynicism—or, if you like, historicism—to justify his *pacifist* convictions. These were solid as a rock. At times they even conflicted with his loyalty to the Communists: he put on his anti-militarist play *Trumpets and Drums* at a time when East Germany, as well as West, was re-arming. It was not the only time he unmistakably called on both the Germanies NOT TO GO AND DO IT AGAIN.

You who live on in towns that passed away
Now show yourselves some mercy, I implore.
Do not go marching into some new war
As if the old wars had not had their day
But show yourselves some mercy, I implore.

You men, reach for the trowel, not the knife.
Today you'd have a roof above your head
Had you not gambled on the knife instead
And with a roof you have a better life.
You men, reach for the trowel, not the knife.

\* \* \*

You mothers, to whom all men owe their breath

A war is yours to give or not to give.
I beg you mothers, let your children live.
Let them owe you their birth but not their death.
I beg you mothers, let your children live.

These verses from "To My Countrymen" belong to Brecht's later years, but the first poem of his that had wide circulation is also a "poem for peace." "Legend of the Dead Soldier" is about the Kaiser and the workings of his draft law in the fifth spring of World War I:

When the fifth spring came and still the war
Made ne'er a pause for breath
The soldier, who knew what a soldier's for,
Died a hero's death.

But war for battle's a synonym
And the Kaiser was most upset
That his soldier had gone and died on him:
He shouldn't have done that—yet.

Without the Kaiser's permission, though,
The summer rolled in like a wave.
Then came a medical commission, oh,
To that young soldier's grave.

This medical commission said
A little prayer to their Maker.
Which done they dug with a holy spade
The soldier from God's little acre.

When the doctor examined the soldier gay
Or what of him was left,
He softly said: This man's 1-A
And he's simply evading the draft.

The soldier was re-inducted.
The night was blue and dry.
If one hadn't had a helmet on one might have detected
The fatherland's stars in the sky.

They filled him up with brandy
Though his flesh had putrefied
And kept two nurses handy
And his half-naked wife at his side.

A priest led a handsome procession there
And knowing corpses well
He flung some incense in the air
To cover up the smell.

Behind the priest there beat and blew
Trumpet and kettle-drum.
The soldier, who knew what he had to do,
Kicked out his legs from his bum.

Zing boom, zing boom, that was the sound
As down the dark streets they did go
And the soldier with them reeling round
Like a stormswept flake of snow.

The cats and dogs, they squeal and prance,
Rats whistle far and near,
For none could bear to belong to France,
Oh fie! the mere idea!

The women came out to see the sight
In the villages near and far.
Trees bowed their heads and the moon shone bright
And everyone cried: Hurrah!

What shouts! What brays! What trumpet peals!
Peasants and priestly flunkey!
And in the middle the soldier reels
Like a drunken monkey.

And up and down, and down and up,
They jostled him till soon
You just couldn't see him except from on top
And there's no one there but the moon.

And the moon won't stay there the whole day through
For the sun can't pause for breath.

The soldier did what he'd been taught to do:
He died a hero's death.*

When I speak of Brecht the pacifist, I am not implying
that he ever espoused nonviolent Gandhiism, but neither
is his pacifism limited to mere protestation against wars.
It led, rather, to a profound study of humanity in war-
time. *Mother Courage* is a panoramic war play with at
least one feature that must be unique in this class of
drama: it contains no battle scenes. It is a play of everyday life at a time like the present—when war was an
everyday fact, and war stands condemned in it not for its
atrocities, but for being itself the supreme atrocity: a
condition of life which should not, must not be tolerated.

In Brecht's world, war is not an isolated iniquity, but
the extreme instance of a universal abuse, the rule of
force. Even those plays of his which stand at the furthest
extreme from communism do not stand at such an extreme from pacifism, because they are studies in force,
in the domination of man by man.

> Force in the hands of another exercises over the soul the
> same tyranny that extreme hunger does; for it possesses,
> and in perpetuo, the power of life and death. Its rule,
> moreover, is as cold and hard as the rule of inert matter.
> The man who knows himself weaker than another is
> more alone in the heart of a city than a man lost in the
> desert.

This is not Bertolt Brecht speaking, but one of the great
religious thinkers of our time, Simone Weil. It comes
closer, however, to describing the world of Brecht than
most of his critics have done. "The man who knows
himself weaker than another is more alone in the heart
of a city than a man lost in the desert." Brecht's very
earliest plays convey just this sense of aloneness in the
heart of the city—that city which Simone Weil calls a
desert and which Brecht called thicket, jungle, and
swamp.

* Copyright © 1958 by Eric Bentley

In one of Brecht's early plays, *In the Swamp*, a man is, in effect, raped by another man. In a play written a little later, a man is, in a social sense, raped by a group of men: this is *A Man's A Man*. *In the Swamp*, we blithely say, is about homosexuality; *A Man's A Man* is a social play, an anti-war play; but, in Brecht, the two things are one. This has even been proved recently by the posthumous publication of a poem from which we learn that the raped man in the two plays was for Brecht the same person. Hence, a Freudian critic might fairly say that the social rape of the later play is a symbol of sexual rape, while a Marxian critic might with equal justice say that the sexual rape of *In the Swamp* prefigures the social rape of *A Man's A Man*. The Marxian point is more interesting, partly because all Brecht's mature plays tend to present social rape, the rape of the innocent individual by a cruel society, partly because for Brecht sex is less a psychic than a social phenomenon (and even loneliness is a matter of feeling "weaker than another"). The reason many people don't readily recognize that *In the Swamp* is about homosexuality is that they are still not accustomed (despite Genet) to seeing sex in terms of a power struggle. In Brecht's "swamp," Garga is the man who "knows himself weaker than another." The play presents the "tyranny" exercised over the soul of Garga by Shlink—and eventually, vice versa —what Brecht calls a boxing match might just as well be called a tug of war.

*A Man's A Man* only narrowly escapes being another play about homosexual rape. It, too, presents a struggle for supremacy between two men, Galy Gay and Bloody Five, and the latter declares in one scene that he'll be raping the former if he isn't given speedy satisfaction by prostitutes—clinically speaking, a classical homosexual pattern of action and fantasy. But the directly sexual material is here pushed even farther into the background. In the foreground is the question of coercion and domination. At the close of *In the Swamp*, we find the dominator dominated—and dead: the plot hinges upon this simple reversal. The tables are similarly turned in *A Man's A Man*. Here, too, the stronger man, the rapist, is in the end discomfited by the weaker, whom he has "raped." In both plays Brecht worries the question: who after all *is* stronger, who weaker? His answer in both cases is that the strong man with an emotional weakness (a weakness for certain emotional "outlets") is less likely to win than the weak man who is willing to deny himself emotional "outlets." Brechtians will recognize here the pattern of some better-known Brecht works, such as *The Seven Deadly Sins* and *The Good Woman of Setzuan*. It was in *A Man's A Man* that Brecht first split characters into contrasting halves. There is Bloody Five, the disciplined soldier, whose discipline disintegrates when he feels sexual passion, and there is Galy Gay who manages to turn from being soft and good to being hard and bad, and so to be the victor in this hard, bad world of ours.

Simple! But underlying the literary and ideological games is the archetypal modern problem: the problem of individual identity. For, though there is nothing modern in the question, *who am I?*, characteristically modern is the lack of *sense* of identity, the feeling of *I am no one* —of which the feeling, *I am more than one person* is a variant. "I am someone, no one, and a hundred thousand people," as one of Pirandello's titles (almost) reads.

Have I wandered far afield? Are pacifism and the problem of identity unconnected? Not at all: the connection is found precisely in such a work as *A Man's A Man*. The protagonist, Galy Gay, brought by the cruel society he lives in to doubt if he has a real identity, accepts a false identity—an identification with precisely the cruelty that is being exerted upon him, with precisely the power that is overpowering him. From a cynical viewpoint, then, he may be said to be effecting a homeopathic self-cure—finding the answer to power in power. Which is surely what those are doing who find the answer to hydrogen bombs in more hydrogen bombs I find myself quoted as having said that *A Man's A Man* is about Madison Avenue. In a sense, it is. Another critic had said the play was about brainwashing. That also, in a sense, is true. But the brainwashing it gives a sense of is that of "Madison Avenue." (Also of "bi-partisan foreign policy"—the idea behind which is to make anyone who dissents feel like a traitor.) Even so one must not *blame* Madison Avenue. Its bullets could not strike home if we were not vulnerable. And the vulnerability consists in our weak sense of identity. Madison Avenue offers a false identity *to those who feel the need of one*.

This interpretation of *A Man's A Man* covers more ground than the avenue between Fifth and Park: it reaches as far as the White House. Power, super-power, atomic power is today offering to fill the terrible void in lives that have no true identity; but this it can never do, since power is itself a void, the supreme void. Hence, total material destruction would be the perfect symbol of our spiritual plight and its most logical consequence, and it is silly to talk as if the holocaust, if it occurred, would be an accident. It is silly to talk as if it were happening because we haven't managed to find a way out. What we confront today is a lack of will to find a way out or, rather, a will not to find the way out: we tend to wish to be destroyed. But, of course, the various statesmen present this cosmic crisis to their respective peoples as a vulgar melodramatic conflict between their own High Ideals and the Low Ideals of their antagonists—and this, to the universal disaster, adds a touch of the ridiculous and the obscene.

All of which brings it about that Bertolt Brecht is a living presence among the American young. I don't say that American youth, as a whole, is of a mind to picket the White House. Such large groups as "American youth" have no mind at all. None the less, there is widespread unrest. It reaches many who neither concur with Castro nor resist the police on Times Square. It is not "pacifist" in the narrower sense of a definite program such as unilateral disarmament, but it IS pacifist in the sense of meaning business in the anti-war movement, and accusing the governments of both Russia and America of not always meaning business in their alleged concern for arms control.

Certainly, the unrest I am speaking of is only a vague, unfocused discontent, grounded in a shrewd suspicion that we are all getting swindled, and that the swindle is leading to universal disaster. Such an attitude is itself quite vulnerable, doubtless, and I might go on to criticize it, were I attempting more than to explain the rapport between young Americans and Bertolt Brecht. This rapport is all the more powerful because somewhat irrational. It is all the more powerful because it is not just a matter of communism. (Parisian Brechtians whose real wish is for communism, will end up espousing communism and dropping Brecht—or explaining with how many reservations they accept him.) It is precisely the Brecht the Communists condemn that young Americans are attracted by—which explains why New York has seen *In the Swamp, Threepenny Opera,* and *A Man's A Man,* and not the later plays. Brecht has become, and will remain, a symbol of malaise and rejection here—and how much more powerful a symbol than the beatnik authors! Or even (to my mind) than Henry Miller or William Burroughs.

But I come back to pacifism because the American Brecht is not *merely* cynical and, in the popular sense, anarchistic. He is anarchistic in a sense closer to the spirit of the great Anarchists. His negatives imply positives. All this hate means love. All this conflict means conciliation. All this war means peace. If we are beginning to conceive, and to build, any alternatives to domination and coercion, it is with the help of Bertolt Brecht.

—E.B.

November 1962

# ADAPTOR'S NOTE

A faithful translation of *A Man's A Man* has already appeared in my *Seven Plays by Bertolt Brecht* (Grove Press, 1961). The present script is the stage version as produced in New York in 1962. Those who are curious about such things are at liberty to compare the two different texts. From the second are missing all passages which could not be made to "work" in a production of the play at Harvard in 1961. During 1961-62 I also was able to polish the dialogue. If it remains eccentric, I tried to make its eccentricity more and more Brechtian. I also made some interpolations. It seemed to me that there should be more Kipling in a version written in Kipling's own language and, since I wanted to write a song for Bloody Five, I made a parody of "Gunga Din." Our audiences have unmistakably found it welcome even when the role is cast with a non-singing actor who delivers it as a recitation. Brecht's original contains but two songs: "A Man's A Man" and "Traveling Bar." I added another or so for the Harvard production, but the show cried out for more still, demanded to be interrupted quite regularly by songs—like later Brecht plays. In the present text there are, in all, seven songs; and, incidentally, I made sure that each main character got one. One of the additional songs is a free translation from a poem by Brecht, "Song of the Three Soldiers," which he himself re-wrote as *Kanonensong* for *The Threepenny Opera*. Hence, four lyrics, qua lyrics, are my own, though often phrases and ideas of Brecht's are embodied in them. My most decisive interpolation is that of the Master of Ceremonies' speeches. These grew out of a discussion with the director of the show. He had been much taken with the "circus" framework of the Berlin production of Brecht's play *Arturo Ui*, and he suggested that *A Man's A Man* could profit from such a framework.

I could not quite see the justification of a circus—or, as later suggested, a carnival—in this play, so I made the counter-suggestion of a military entertainment in aid of a recruiting drive. Cuba had recently been invaded. Our Attorney General was saying that atomic weapons would be used, if need be, in defense of Berlin. *A Man's A Man* could be presented as an ironical recruiting poster. I am speaking of the Harvard production—summer 1961. The political situation a year later, when the New York production was prepared, was different—but not very. I kept the framework, shifting the emphasis slightly to give more weight to the problem of identity. This represented a slight geographic shift, too: New York is the city of Madison Avenue, the avenue of false identities. Hence the Recruiting Song reflects New York. But it is to be feared that New York reflects modernity in general. As "Johnny Jones" has it in the play:

There was a time when priest and pedagogue besought me
To think that I was I and you were you.
The very songs my dear old mother taught me
Said: Be yourself! And: To thyself be true!
But later on a million brothers told me:
You are not you, I am by no means I.
And this the gospel that my brothers sold me:
Be someone else! Be Tommy! Go on: try!

Finally, there is one difference between my translation and my adaptation which may be mystifying to those who are innocent of the exigencies of theatre: The word *elephant* has sometimes been changed to *squirrel*. The reason is that the word is used to describe the figure of the actor playing Galy Gay. Unless, therefore, one could cast the role with Mr. Zero Mostel, one is faced with an incongruity. If one's Galy Gay is delicately built, he becomes a squirrel! Something, of course, is thereby lost. The whole play can be regarded as an elephant fable. After all, the idea of making a fake elephant in the climactic scene stems from someone's calling Galy Gay an elephant. He is an elephant again in the "Pal Jacky" interlude (though that is not usually played). And Brechtian *aficionados* will point out that Baal, another early Brecht protagonist, is also elephantine, and that, as late as *The Good Woman of Setzuan,* Brecht tells a variant of the Galy Gay story in his "Song of the Eighth Elephant." . . . But it seems that Galy Gay has never yet been played by a Falstaffian actor: men with that figure so seldom have the talent, and in the theatre talented squirrels must always be given priority over dumb elephants.

—E.B.

# A MAN'S A MAN

A comedy with songs

by

Bertolt Brecht

Adapted by Eric Bentley

# CAST

in order of appearance

MASTER OF CEREMONIES
AGATHA BEGBICK ⎫
JENNY BEGBICK ⎬ *Widow Begbick's Jazz Band*
JOBIA BEGBICK ⎭
PRIVATE JOHNNY JONES
CORPORAL SOLLY SCHMITT
GALY GAY
MRS. GAY
URIAH SHELLEY ⎫
JERAIAH JIP ⎪
POLLY BAKER ⎬ *A Machine-Gun Unit*
JESSE MAHONEY ⎭
MISTER WANG
WIDOW LEOCADIA BEGBICK
BLOODY FIVE
SOLDIERS

THE PLACE: India
THE TIME: The nineteen-twenties perhaps

First produced at the Masque Theatre, 442 West 42nd Street, New York City, September 19th, 1962, by the New Repertory Theatre Company, directed by John Hancock, Music by Joseph Raposo, with the following cast:

| | | |
|---|---|---|
| POLLY ........................... | | Clifton James |
| JENNY BEGBICK | | Susan Cogan |
| AGATHA BEGBICK | *Daughters of Begbick* | Edith Valentine |
| JOBIA BEGBICK | | Maggie Ziskind |
| JERAIAH JIP ..................... | | Konrad Matthaei |
| WIDOW LEOCADIA BEGBICK .......... | | Olympia Dukakis |
| GALY GAY ....................... | | John Heffernan |
| MRS. GAY ........................ | | Buzzi |
| URIAH .......................... | | Harvey Solin |
| JESSE .......................... | | Ken Kercheval |
| WANG .......................... | | Maurice Edwards |
| BLOODY FIVE .................... | | Michael Conrad |
| SOLDIERS ............. | | David Tress, David Spielberg, Eric Berger, Michael Quinn, Louis Quinones |
| SEXTON ......................... | | Earle Edgerton |
| SOLLY SCHMITT .................. | | Maurice Edwards |

# PROLOGUE

*Calliope music. Enter a* MASTER OF CEREMONIES *in military uniform.*

MASTER OF CEREMONIES: This evening's entertainment is brought to you by His Majesty's Imperial Indian Army. Are you a civilian? You need not remain one long. Are you a homebody? Do you love your wife? All this can be taken care of. You can become a fighter, a 100% he-man. You can forget there ever was such a thing as hearth and home. Only pay careful attention to our story, the story of Galy Gay, a homey sort of fellow, a loyal and loving husband, but transformed, nay transfigured, at last, into a citizen, a patriot, a soldier, a builder of empire. All proceeds to His Majesty's Recruiting campaign. Within a matter of weeks, it may be necessary to invade Tibet, Afghanistan, Burma, and all points east. Are you doing your bit? Are you on the road to Mandalay? Note the recruiting booth in the lobby of this theatre. Or, if you prefer, you may come forward and join up publicly, here on this stage, at any point during the performance. Every nice girl loves a soldier, your king and country need you, join the army and see the world—classic slogans! Never shall they die! You'll die but they won't. They only need from time to time the slightest adjustment to new circumstances, for this is the 20th century, the army's century, the unique century—unique because it's the only one that will never get up to a hundred. And now before our story begins, "Recruiting Song," the recruiting song of the twentieth century! (*He introduces the* PLAYERS *and* SINGERS *to the audience as they enter.*) Agatha Begbick! Jenny Begbick! Jobia Begbick! Private Johnny Jones! Corporal Solly Schmitt! Johnny!

### Recruiting Song

JOHNNY JONES:

There was a time when yes was yes and no was no
When Jones was Jones and Schmitt was only Schmitt
When black was black and snow was only snow
And I was I, you you, when it was it.
But nowadays we sing another song.
The keynote now is relativity.
And left is right, and right is mostly wrong.
When he's a she, what will become of me?

SOLLY SCHMITT:

Join the army, Johnny,
We're off to Calcutta tonight!
Snow isn't snow, Johnny,
And black is white.
Pack your kitbag, Johnny,
And fight, fight, fight,
For right is wrong, Johnny,
And might is right.

# 1

## KILKOA

*Projection:* SEE INDIA FROM AN AISLE SEAT! IN THE SEA-PORT OF OLD KILKOA, THE WATERFRONT PORTER GALY GAY COMES TO A CONCLUSION.

GALY GAY *and* MRS. GAY.

GALY GAY: My dearest wife, I have come to a conclusion: I am going out to buy a fish. Such a purchase, after all, is not beyond the means of a waterfront porter who doesn't drink, smokes very little and has very few vices. Now: shall I buy a big fish, or will a little one do?

MRS. GAY: A little one will do.

GALY GAY: What kind of a fish shall I buy?

MRS. GAY: How about a nice little flounder? But no. On second thoughts, don't buy a fish. Stay home. For the fishwives are lewd and on the lookout for men, and you have a soft heart, Galy Gay.

GALY GAY: True. But a waterfront porter has nothing. They'll leave me in peace.

MRS. GAY: Then there are these soldiers. Terrible fellows. And arriving in hordes at the railway station, so I hear. Why, the market place must be swarming with them already, and we're lucky if they aren't committing burglary and murder all over town. Galy Gay, you'd better stay indoors.

GALY GAY: They won't do anything to just a waterfront porter.

MRS. GAY: Galy Gay, Galy Gay, you can run like a squirrel, but you're small like a squirrel, and delicate like a squirrel. Keep out of harm's way, Galy Gay.

GALY GAY: Your husband is a match for any soldier.

MRS. GAY: Yes, for one. Maybe even for two. And, by a little stretch of the imagination, for three. But, husband, these fellows go around in fours.

GALY GAY: That's enough. I came to a conclusion, and I'll stick to it. Put the water on for the fish: I'm working up an appetite. I'll be back in ten minutes. (*He leaves.*)

MRS. GAY (*calling after him*): Well, be very careful! And no loitering around! (*To the audience:*) And so he needn't worry about any stray soldiers in these parts, I'm going to lock myself in the kitchen.

# 2

## STREET BESIDE THE OLD PAGODA OF THE YELLOW MONKS

*Projection:* LAND OF MAHARAJAHS AND PAGAN TEMPLES! BEFORE THE OLD PAGODA OF THE YELLOW MONKS A BRITISH MACHINE-GUN UNIT MEETS WITH A SETBACK.

*Four soldiers:* URIAH SHELLEY, JESSE MAHONEY, POLLY BAKER, *and* JERAIAH JIP *on their way to camp.*

URIAH: Polly Baker!
POLLY: Polly Baker!
URIAH: Jeraiah Jip!
JIP: Jeraiah Jip!
URIAH: Jesse Mahoney!
JESSE: Jesse Mahoney!
URIAH: Uriah Shelley. The machine-gun unit, which has been called The Scum, and which has been stationed in the city of Kankerdan, has now arrived, intact, in the seaport of Kilkoa. In celebration of which, we shall sing our song, "The Song of The Scum." (*And they do.*)

*The Song of The Scum*
John joined up, and so did James,
And George's medals stretched from here to here.
But let's not make a fuss about their names:
They were marching to the Northwest Frontier.
    We love our neighbor
    With gun and saber
    From the Congo to Ceylon.
    If it should rain one night
    And we should chance to fight
    The brown or yellow faces

Of the inferior races
We'll slice them up to make some tasty
Filet mignon.

John got killed, and James dropped dead,
And George, so rumor had it, went plain barmy.
But blood, my hearties, blood, is still blood red:
THEY'RE RECRUITING ONCE AGAIN FOR
THE ARMY.

Today our mission
Is nuclear fission:
Hail to thee, Atomic Bomb!
If our filet mignon
Is slightly overdone
We'll smash the ugly faces
Of the inferior races
And blow the disunited nations
To Kingdom Come!*

JESSE: Just as the mighty tanks of our King must be
filled with gasoline, so they can be seen riding the
goddamned roads of this all-too-endless Eldorado,
even so indispensable, to the British soldier, is the
drinking of whisky.

JIP: How much whisky have we got left?

POLLY: We are four. We have five bottles. We need
eleven more bottles.

JESSE: We need money.

URIAH: There are people who have something against
soldiers, but a single one of these pagodas contains
more copper than it takes to send a regiment from
Calcutta to London.

POLLY: The hint our dear friend Uriah has given us con-

---

* It is an old tradition of the European theatre that new and
topical tags can be added to old songs and, for that matter, Brecht
himself has written a set of new words for *The Threepenny Opera*,
replete with references to the Nazis, etcetera. I have followed in
this tradition here, and also in "The Song of the Ganges River."
—E. B.

cerning a pagoda which is dilapidated and covered with fly-shit but which may also be stuffed full of copper certainly merits our most serious attention.

JIP: For my part, I've got to have more to drink, Polly.

URIAH: Patience, my friend. This Asia has a hole: one can crawl through it.

JIP: Uriah, Uriah, you know what my mother used to tell me? "Do anything you like, dearly beloved Jeraiah, but beware of pitch." And around here it smells of pitch.

POLLY: The door's not shut.

JESSE: Careful, Polly, there's sure to be some devilment behind it.

URIAH: What are these windows for? Let's fish for poor boxes. This way. (*He leans through the window and lowers the belt on the inside.*)

POLLY: Got something?

URIAH: No: my helmet fell in.

POLLY: Hell, you can't go back to camp without your helmet!

URIAH: Oho, the things I'm fishing up! What an establishment! Just look! Rat traps! Man traps!

JESSE: Let's give up. This is no ordinary temple. This is a trap.

URIAH: A temple's a temple: I've got to get my helmet back.

JIP: How?

*Pause. They look at each other. A wire catches POLLY's eye. He takes it for a rope.*

POLLY: What have we here? A rope.

JESSE: I could do my morning exercises on that rope.

URIAH: Try it.

*JESSE bends each terrible agent to this terrible feat. But the wire has a fire alarm attached to it and gives off smoke, light, and fire. After receiving an electric shock, JESSE is silent but surly.*

127

POLLY: Let me make an observation. The door of this pagoda is not shut.

JESSE: Further dangers, however, may lurk in a pagoda like that.

URIAH: Exactly. Give me your identity cards. Identity cards must in no way and at no time be damaged. And why not? Because a man can be replaced any time but nothing is sacred any more unless it's identity cards.

*They hand in their cards as they enter through the door.*

JIP: Jeraiah Jip.

POLLY: Polly Baker.

JESSE: Jesse Mahoney.

URIAH: Uriah Shelley. And now: forward into battle. With, of course, a minimum of *noticeable* damage. The Army has its reputation to think of.

JIP *is left behind.* MR. WANG *is seen at a window.*

JIP: Oh. Good morning. Are you the owner? Nice place you've got there.

URIAH: Pass the bread knife, Jesse: I propose to break open these poor boxes.

*Horrendous noises from inside the temple.* JIP *goes in through the door. The three come out above, pale, in rags, bleeding.*

POLLY: This calls for revenge.

URIAH: This temple has no conception of fair play. What animals!

POLLY: Blood must flow.

JIP (*from inside*): Hey!

URIAH: Now I shoot up the whole caboodle.
*The three climb down and aim the machine gun at the pagoda.*

POLLY: Fire!

JIP: Hey! What are you all doing?

POLLY: Where are you hiding out?

JIP: Here.

JESSE: What are you doing in that rat trap anyway?

JIP: I came for the money. It's here.

URIAH: The biggest drunk among us finds it right off. (*Loudly:*) Come out—through this door.

JIP (*sticks out his head above*): Where?

URIAH: Through this door.

JIP: Ouch! What's this?

POLLY: What's wrong with him?

JIP: Just look!

URIAH: Something else?

JIP: My hair! Ow! My hair! I can't move forward! And I can't move backward! Ow! My hair! It's fastened to something! Uriah, find out what my hair's stuck to! Ow! Uriah, cut me loose! I'm hanging by the hair!

URIAH: Jesse, your bread knife to cut him loose!

*This is done.*

POLLY: And now he has a bald patch. Everyone will recognize him.

JESSE: A Wanted Sign in human form.

URIAH: A bald patch will betray us. (*Points to a palanquin:*) Lay him in that palanquin. I'll return this evening and shave the whole of his head so there'll be no bald patch. (*He gives them their identity cards back.*) Jesse Mahoney!

JESSE (*taking his card*): Jesse Mahoney.

URIAH: Polly Baker!

POLLY (*taking his card*): Polly Baker.

URIAH: Jeraiah Jip. (JIP *starts to rise.*) I'll keep this. (URIAH *pockets his identity card:*) Sit inside that thing and wait.

*The three leave.* MR. WANG *is seen inspecting the hair that is stuck in the doorway.*

# HIGHWAY BETWEEN KILKOA AND THE CAMP

*Projection:* SEE A REAL LIVE TIGER, THE TIGER OF KILKOA, ALSO KNOWN AS SERGEANT CHARLES ("BLOODY FIVE") FAIRCHILD!

BLOODY FIVE, *a Sergeant, steps out from behind a tree and hangs a* Wanted *sign on it.*

BLOODY FIVE: Nothing in a very long time has struck me as so strange, me, Sergeant Charles Fairchild of His Majesty's Indian Army, alias the Human Typhoon, alias the Tiger of Kilkoa, denominated on less happy occasions The Bloody Gent, but, in general, Bloody Five, and, among intimates, just plain Bloody! (*He points to the sign with one finger.*) Burglary at the Pagoda of the Yellow Monks. Clue to the mystery: a quarter pound of hair embedded in pitch on the scene of the crime. Somewhere there must be a man with a bald patch in a machine-gun unit. That would be the guilty party. Simple! But who comes here? (*He steps behind the tree.*)

POLLY, URIAH, *and* JESSE *enter and are appalled to see the sign.*

BLOODY FIVE (*stepping forward*): You've seen a man with a bald patch, haven't you?

POLLY: No.

BLOODY FIVE: Your appearance! You look like you'd just had breakfast in an ant heap. How about taking your helmets off? And where's your fourth man?

URIAH: Answering a call of nature, Sergeant.

BLOODY FIVE: Then let's wait and ask him if *he* hasn't seen a man with a bald patch.

*They wait.*

Quite a long call of nature.

JESSE: Maybe he's gone back another way.

BLOODY FIVE: We shall take roll call. And should you come to roll call without your fourth man, you will wish, let me tell you, that martial law had been declared in your mother's wombs and that you had duly shot each other according to the book of rules. (*Exit.*)

URIAH: Before the drum sounds for roll call, we've got to have a fourth man.

POLLY: I hope this isn't our sergeant. If this rattlesnake is taking roll call we might as well stand with our backs to the wall right now, Uriah. Here comes a man. Let's secretly observe him.

*They hide. Enter* GALY GAY *in the wake of* WIDOW BEGBICK. *He carries her basket of cucumbers.*

BEGBICK: This road is very little frequented. A woman might have a hard time of it here—vis-à-vis any man who might wish to embrace her.

GALY GAY: As the owner of a canteen, you have to deal with soldiers every day of the week. They're the worst of men. I imagine you've learned how to wrestle with them.

BEGBICK: Oh, sir, you should never say things like that to a woman. There are certain words, my dear sir, that bring women to the point where their blood tingles.

GALY GAY: I'm just an ordinary waterfront porter.

BEGBICK: Roll call for the new recruits is due in a few minutes. The drums are rolling already, as you can hear. There'll be no one on the road.

GALY GAY: If it's really so late, I must hurry back to Kilkoa: I still have a fish to buy.

BEGBICK: Permit me one question, Mister, if I heard your name right, Galy Gay: is great strength needed in the porter's profession?

GALY GAY: I wouldn't have believed I could be held up

nearly ten hours by unforeseen interruptions from just buying a fish and going home. But once I get rolling I'm like a passenger train!

BEGBICK: It is, of course, one thing to buy a fish to fill your belly, and quite another to help a lady carry her basket. But the lady might know how to show her gratitude in a manner that outweighs the pleasure of eating fish.

GALY GAY: Frankly, I just want to go and buy a fish.

BEGBICK: I quite understand, sir. But don't you think it's been getting late? The shops are shut, and all the fish are sold.

GALY GAY: I have an imagination, let me tell you. For example, I've often had enough of a fish before I've even seen it. But some people have their fish many times over. They go to buy it, then they do buy it, then they carry it home, then they cook it to a turn, then they wolf it down, and even then, when they're in bed at night, and think they have written finis to the chapter entitled Digestion, that sad little fish is still keeping them busy. All because they have no imagination.

BEGBICK: I have a suggestion. For the money you were going to buy a fish with, buy this cucumber. To oblige you, I'll lower the price.

GALY GAY: But I don't need a cucumber.

BEGBICK: Well, I certainly didn't think you'd shame me like this!

GALY GAY: It's just that the water's on for the fish.

BEGBICK: Have it your own way, have it your own way.

GALY GAY: Please believe me when I say I should very much like to oblige you.

BEGBICK: It's clear that when you open your mouth, you only put your foot in it.

GALY GAY: I certainly mustn't disappoint you. If you still want to let the cucumber go for less, the money will be found.

URIAH (*to* JESSE *and* POLLY): This is a man who can't say no.

GALY GAY: Careful. There are soldiers around.

BEGBICK: Heaven knows what they're after: it's just before roll call. Give me my basket quick. There would seem to be little point in my gossiping the time away with you a moment longer. (*Exit.*)

URIAH: This is our man.

JESSE: A man who can't say no.

POLLY: He even has red hair like good old Jip. (*He steps forward.*)

JESSE: Never look a gift horse in the *mouth,* it may be an ass.

POLLY: Nice evening, this evening.

GALY GAY: Yes, sir, it is.

POLLY: Look, it's very remarkable, sir, but I can't get the idea out of my head that you must be from Kilkoa.

GALY GAY: Kilkoa? Of course. There stands my little hut, so to speak.

POLLY: I'm very, very happy to hear it, Mister . . .

GALY GAY: Galy Gay.

POLLY: Yes, you have a little hut there, haven't you?

GALY GAY: And that's how you happen to know me? Or maybe you know my wife?

POLLY: Your name, yes, your name is, just a moment, Galy Gay.

GALY GAY: Quite right. That *is* my name.

POLLY: I knew it. That's me all over. For instance, I'll take a bet you're married. But why are we just standing around, Mister Galy Gay? These are my friends Jesse and Uriah. Come over to the canteen and smoke a pipe with us!

GALY GAY: Thank you. But my wife is expecting me in Kilkoa. And silly as it may seem, I haven't got a pipe.

POLLY: A cigar then. You can't beg off now, can you, it's such a lovely evening.

GALY GAY: No, that's right, now I can't say no.

POLLY: And you'll get your cigar too.

*All four leave.*

133

# 4

## CANTEEN OF WIDOW LEOCADIA BEGBICK

*Projection:* SEE INDIA! ALL OF INDIA! THE TAJ MAHAL HAS
NOTHING ON WIDOW BEGBICK'S TRAVELING BAR.

SOLDIERS. *To them,* WIDOW BEGBICK.

BEGBICK: Good evening, soldiers all! I am Widow Begbick, and this is my beer wagon. Hooked up to the
giant troop trains, it rides every railway track in
India. And because you can drink as you ride, yes,
at one and the same time, and because you even
sleep as you ride, this beer wagon is called Widow
Begbick's Traveling Bar. And from Hyderabad to
Rangoon everyone knows how many soldier boys
have found refuge in it when they just weren't being
treated right. Accompanied by my daughters, Widow
Begbick's World Famous Jazz Band, I shall now
sing the Song of the Traveling Bar.

*Song of the Traveling Bar*

From Samarkand to Kandahar
Leocadia Begbick's your best friend
And in her celebrated Traveling Bar
You can smoke and sleep and drink for years on end.
    From Bangalore to Mandalay
    When a fellow can't be found all day
    They say he's down the whisky well,
    With cocktails, gum and hi hi hi
    On the road past heaven, on the rim of hell,
    Keep your mouth shut, Tommy, keep your
                        hair on, Tommy,
    From the soda mountain to the whisky well.

In Widow Begbick's Traveling Bar
You can get just what you want, by gum.
This wagon rolled through good old Indiah
When the drink you drank came from your dear
old mum.

From Bangalore to Mandalay
When a fellow can't be found all day
They say he's down the whisky well,
With cocktails, gum, and hi hi hi
On the road past heaven, on the rim of hell,
Keep your mouth shut, Tommy, keep your
hair on, Tommy,
From the soda mountain to the whisky well.

And when battle roars through the Punjab Vale
And the niggers form their nigger front
We smoke and sleep and drink her nutbrown ale:
The hunt is up! The bloody nigger hunt!
From Bangalore to Mandalay
When a fellow can't be found all day
They say he's down the whisky well,
With cocktails, gum, and hi hi hi
On the road past heaven, on the rim of hell
Keep your mouth shut, Tommy, keep your
hair on, Tommy,
From the soda mountain to the whisky well.

Now, Jobia, take up the collection, will you, my
dear, or the pigs will wriggle out of it. But do it
politely, O flower on the soldier's dusty path.
JOBIA: Why? (*She takes up the collection.*)

*Enter the three and* GALY GAY.

URIAH: Is this the canteen of the Eighth Regiment?
SOLDIER: It is.
SECOND SOLDIER: Are there only three of you?
THIRD SOLDIER: Where's your fourth man?
URIAH: What sort of man is the sergeant?

FOURTH SOLDIER: Not too nice.

POLLY: That's unfortunate. That the sergeant is not too nice.

JOBIA: Name: Charles Fairchild. *Nom de guerre:* Bloody Five. Honorary Titles: the Human Typhoon, the Tiger of Kilkoa, etcetera.

JENNY: And when a man's time has come, when they're ready to stand him up against the wall and it's a miracle he doesn't wet his pants like a baby, which is why it is called the Johnny-are-your-pants-dry-wall, Bloody Five gives vent to the following battle cry: "Pack your kit bag, Johnny."

AGATHA: They say he has an unnatural sense of smell, he has a nose for crime, and when he smells a crime, he sings: "Pack your kit bag, Johnny."

FIRST SOLDIER: Yes, you'll soon see what the score is in Kilkoa.

POLLY (*to* GALY GAY): My dear sir, you are in a position to do a small favor to three poor soldiers in their hour of need and without going to any special trouble either. Our fourth man, what with saying good-bye to his wife, is late, and if there aren't four of us at roll call, we shall be thrown into the black dungeons of Kilkoa. It would therefore be a help if you would put on one of our uniforms, stand by when they number off the new arrivals, and call out his name. That would be all. Don't let a cigar more or less that you may possibly be smoking at our expense influence your decision.

GALY GAY: It isn't that I wouldn't very much like to oblige you but unfortunately I must rush home. I cannot act as I might wish to.

POLLY: Our heartfelt thanks. I freely admit I expected it of you. Yes. You cannot do what you'd like to do. You'd like to go home but you cannot go home. Our heartfelt thanks, sir: the confidence we placed in you at first sight was fully merited.

JESSE: Your hand, sir.

URIAH: To this end, allow us to robe you in the venerable vestments of the British Army. (*He rings.* BEGBICK *comes in.*)

POLLY: Are we addressing the owner of the camp canteen, the world-famous Widow Begbick? We are a machine-gun unit of the Eighth Regiment. May I be open with you, Widow Begbick? (*He whispers something in her ear.*)

BEGBICK: I see. You've lost a complete set of regimentals?

POLLY: Yes, while our friend Jip was in the bath house, some Chink made off with his uniform.

BEGBICK: I see. In the bath house?

SECOND SOLDIER: And now it's ours.

THIRD SOLDIER: They call them The Scum, those four.

FOURTH SOLDIER: Their crimes shall follow them like their shadows.

FIFTH SOLDIER: And just behind them: a Wanted Sign.

BEGBICK *comes back with the regimentals.*

JESSE: To be open, wide open, with you, Widow Begbick, it has to do with a little joke.

BEGBICK: I see. A little joke?

POLLY: Isn't that about it, dear sir? A little joke?

GALY GAY: Yes, yes, it has to do, so to speak, with—a cigar. (*He laughs. The three laugh too.*)

BEGBICK: How helpless a weak woman is beside three strong men! No one shall say of Widow Begbick that she wouldn't let a man change his trousers.

GALY GAY (*quickly*): What goes on? Actually?

JESSE: Actually—nothing at all.

*All four laugh.*

GALY GAY: Isn't it dangerous—when they find out?

POLLY: Not a bit. Anyhow, in your case just once is the same as not at all.

GALY GAY: That's true. They do say just once is the same as not at all.

SOLDIER: This is the famous machine-gun unit that decided the outcome of the battle of Hyderabad.

POLLY: This is the venerable vestment we are buying for you. Try it on, Brother Galy Gay.

POLLY *and* URIAH *put it on* GALY GAY.

BEGBICK: It'll cost you ten shillings, I'm giving it away.

POLLY: Ten shillings!

URIAH: Bloodsucker! We'll pay three at the most. It's much too small, too.

JESSE (*at the window*): Rain clouds all of a sudden! If it rains now, the palanquin will be wet, and if the palanquin is wet, it will be taken into the pagoda, and if it is taken into the pagoda, Jip will be discovered, and if Jip is discovered, the jig is up.

GALY GAY: Too small. I'll never get into it.

POLLY: Hear that? He'll never get into it.

GALY GAY: And the shoes pinch terribly.

URIAH: Everything's too small—not usable! Two shillings!

POLLY: Quiet, Uriah. Seven shillings, because everything's too small, and the shoes pinch, isn't that so?

GALY GAY: Out of the ordinary. They pinch extremely.

URIAH: This gentleman is not so easygoing as you, Polly.

BEGBICK: Eight shillings. Or the company will get wind of the crime specified on that sign. Shitpots!

JESSE: Think it's going to rain, Widow Begbick?

BEGBICK: Well now, I must take a look at Sergeant Bloody Five.

JESSE: Why?

BEGBICK: I was forgetting you don't know the sergeant. Well, in time of rainfall, he's subject to attacks of acute sensuality.

JESSE: No!

BEGBICK: Yes! He's completely changed, inside and out.

JESSE: It mustn't rain on any account—because of our joke.

BEGBICK: On the contrary. It need only start raining, and Bloody Five, the most dangerous man in the Indian

Army, is as mild as a milk-tooth. For, when it rains, Bloody Five is transformed into the Bloody Gent, and the Bloody Gent concentrates on girls for three days on end.

SOLDIER (*entering to make an announcement*): Everybody report for roll call! It's this Pagoda business. They say there's a man missing, so they're going to call the roll, and examine identity cards. (*Exit.*)

JESSE (*to* GALY GAY): All you have to do is call out our lost comrade's name. As loud as possible and very distinct. It's nothing!

POLLY: And our lost comrade's name is Jeraiah Jip.

GALY GAY (*politely*): Jeraiah Jip.

POLLY: It is pleasant to meet cultured gentlemen who know how to behave in every situation.

*The four leave at the back, each of them bowing.*

JESSE (*leaving*): If only it doesn't rain!

BEGBICK: And now there stands up in the ranks, before the very eyes of Bloody Five, a man who isn't a soldier of any kind! And the porter Galy Gay is a special sort of man at that. Here comes Bloody Five.

JOBIA: The sergeant looks like he's got a bayonet in his pants' pocket, why *is* that?

*Enter* BLOODY FIVE, *frightfully changed.*

BEGBICK (*looks at him*): The Bloody Gent! Jobia, quick: put the awning up: it's going to rain!

BLOODY FIVE (*while the Eighth Regiment call their names*): You laugh, but I tell you I'd like to see the whole thing go up in flames, this Sodom of the rocking chair and whisky bar, and you with it, for you're a Gomorrah in yourself, you gobble me up when you look at me like that, you whitewashed Babylon!

BEGBICK: You know, Charlie, a woman enjoys seeing a man in such a passionate mood!

BLOODY FIVE: The human race began to disintegrate the

first time some muttonhead failed to button up. As literature, the army field manual may have its shortcomings, but what else can a man fall back on, if he *is* a man? It takes all the responsibility. Actually, I'd be for digging a hole in the ground, sticking some dynamite in it, and blowing the whole world to blazes! Then maybe they'd find out we meant business.

OFFICER'S VOICE (*outside, giving orders*): Machine gunners! Call! Names!

BLOODY FIVE (*humming*): "Pack you kit bag, Johnny!" (*Now he hears* URIAH, POLLY, *and* JESSE *call their names.*) Yes, and now: a short pause.

GALY GAY'S VOICE: Jeraiah Jip.

BLOODY FIVE: They've cooked something up.

BEGBICK: I tell you, Sergeant, before the black rain of Nepal has been falling for two nights on end, you will be more gently disposed to the misdeeds of mankind. For you are perhaps the sexiest man beneath the sun. And you will sit down at table with insubordination, and the desecrators of the temple will look you straight in the eye, for your crimes will be as numberless as the sands of the sea.

BLOODY FIVE: Yes, but then we'd see a little action. Make no mistake, my love, we would then take action against little old Bloody Five, and no half measures about it. It's as simple as that. (*Exit. Outside:*) Eight men up to the navel in hot sand for not having regulation haircuts!

*Enter* URIAH, POLLY, *and* JESSE *with* GALY GAY, *to the bar.*

POLLY: A glass of whisky to your health, sir!

GALY GAY: Oh, a little favor—man to man, so to speak—can never hurt. I'm drinking whisky like it was water and saying to myself: I did these gentlemen a good turn. Isn't that what really matters in this world? You send up a little balloon—"Jeraiah Jip" is no harder to say than "Good evening"—and you're just the man people wish you to be—easy!

POLLY: Unhappily we're in a hurry. A dangerous rain wind has blown up. And, you see, we must shave someone's head.

GALY GAY: Couldn't I help with that too?

URIAH: Some people have to stick their noses into everything. Give such people your little finger, and they grab your whole hand.

POLLY: Drink several cocktails at our expense. (*Leaving:*) When we've gone to work on Jip's head with these scissors, he won't have any bald patch any more. Only it mustn't rain, that's all. It mustn't rain.

*Exeunt the three.*

BEGBICK (*brings a cocktail for* GALY GAY): Haven't we met before, this evening?

GALY GAY *shakes his head.*

Isn't your name Galy Gay?

GALY GAY *shakes his head.*

Aren't you the man who carried my cucumber basket?

GALY GAY: No. I am not.

BEGBICK: It's started to rain.

GALY GAY *goes to sleep.* BEGBICK *smokes a pipe and reads the Times.*

The London *Times* informs me and my daughters
What great men do in countries various.
I would not meet such men at closer quarters.
My favorite pleasures are vicarious.
Let others make the headlines on page one:
I am the everlasting looker-on.
(*Singing:*)

Song of the Ganges River
I was born on the rug in a Dublin snug

And grew up with heroic desires.
In old Ireland's cause I'd have broken all laws
And perished in Protestant fires.
Yet nowadays I have no wish to die
(Leastways not prematurely)
And when heroes commend a sensational end
I answer them slowly but surely:
    Take a look at the Ganges River
    As it sweeps from Benares to the sea.
    Can I swim against that current? Never.
    Who'd even make a stab at it? Not me.
    Why should I join you in your derring-do?
    I'm happy sitting here admiring you.

Columbus, he did sail the sea.
    Lindbergh, he flew above it.
Some fellow soon will set foot on the moon
    And more than likely love it.
Now I do not despise the moon in the skies
    Or regard it with derision.
But I simply won't race into outer space:
    I shall watch it on television.
    Take a look at the Ganges River
    As it sweeps from Benares to the sea.
    Could I swim against that current? Never.
    Who'd even make a stab at it? Not me.
    Why should I risk my neck with Colonel Glenn
    When I can see it all on Channel Ten?

# 5

## INSIDE THE PAGODA OF THE YELLOW MONKS

*Projection:* METAMORPHOSIS NUMBER ONE. A MAN TURNS INTO A GOD.

MISTER WANG *and his Chinese* SEXTON.

SEXTON: It's raining.

WANG: Bring our palanquin in where it's dry.

*Exit* SEXTON.

And now our last source of income has been stolen. And it's raining on my head through those holes.

*The* SEXTON *drags in the palanquin. Groans from inside it.*

What's that? (*He looks in.*) I knew it. I knew it would be a white man when I saw how filthy the palanquin was. Oh dear, he's in soldier's uniform. And he has a bald patch, the thief. They simply cut his hair off. What shall we do with him? He's a soldier, so he won't have any sense. A soldier of the queen, covered with vomited liquor, helpless as a barnyard chick, and so drunk his own mother wouldn't know him! One could make a present of him to the police. But what good is that? When your money's all gone, what good is justice? And all he can do is grunt. (*Furiously, to the* SEXTON:) Pick him up and stuff him in the prayer box, you hole in a Swiss cheese! And see that his head sticks out at the top. The best thing we can do is make a god out of him.

*The* SEXTON *puts* JIP *in the prayer box.*

Bring me paper! We must hang paper banners in front of the house without delay! We must paint some posters! I want this to be on the grand scale! No false economies! These must be posters no one can overlook! What good is a god if he doesn't get talked about?

POLLY: Hello!

WANG: Who's that at my door so late?

POLLY: Three soldiers.

WANG: His comrades. (*He lets the three in.*)

POLLY: We're looking for a man—a soldier, I should say—who is fast asleep in a palanquin which was right in front of this rich and noble temple.

WANG: May his awakening be a pleasant one!

POLLY: But, you see, this palanquin has vanished.

WANG: I understand your impatience: it proceeds from uncertainty. I myself am looking for several people—in all about three people—soldiers, I should say—and I cannot find them.

URIAH: It'll be hard. I think you may as well give up. But we thought you might know something about the palanquin.

WANG: Alas, no. The unpleasant fact is that all you soldiers of the king wear the same clothes.

JESSE: It isn't unpleasant. There's a man in the aforementioned palanquin who is very sick.

POLLY: Having also lost some hair through this illness, he urgently needs help.

URIAH: Would you have seen some such man?

WANG: Alas no! But I have found some such hair. However, a sergeant from your army took it. To return it to its rightful soldier.

JIP *groans from inside the prayer box.*

POLLY: What is that, sir?

WANG: A milch cow. Fast asleep.

URIAH: A milch cow that sleeps badly, it seems.

POLLY: This is the palanquin we stuffed Jip into. Permit us to examine it.

WANG: It is best if I tell you the whole truth. That, you see, is another palanquin.

POLLY: It's as full of vomit as a spittoon on the third day of Christmas. Jesse, Jip was in there.

WANG: Not so. He cannot have been. No one would sit in such a dirty palanquin.

JIP *in the prayer box groans loudly.*

URIAH: We must have a fourth man if we slaughter our grandmothers to get him.

WANG: The man you are looking for is not here. But that you may see that the man, who you say is here—and whom I do not know to be here—is not your man, permit me to explain it all to you with the aid of a drawing. Allow your unworthy servant to draw four criminals with chalk. (*He draws them on the door of the prayer box.*) One of them has a face, so that one sees who he is, but three of them have no faces. They cannot be recognized. Yet the one with the face has no money, therefore he is no thief. But the ones with the money have no faces, therefore they cannot be recognized. That's how it is as long as they are not together. But when they are together the three headless men grow faces, and other people's money will be found in their pockets. I would never be able to believe you if you said that a man who might be found here was your man.

*The three threaten him with their weapons, but at a sign from* WANG *the* SEXTON *appears with* CHINESE VISITORS *to the temple.*

JESSE: We wouldn't wish to disturb your rest any longer, sir. Also, your tea does not agree with us. On the other hand, your drawing is a work of art. Let's go!

WANG: It hurts me to see you leave.

URIAH: Ten horses won't be able to stop our comrade coming back to us—wherever he may be when he wakes. Or don't you agree?

WANG: Perhaps ten horses won't. But perhaps one small part of one horse will. Who knows?

URIAH: As soon as he's got the whisky out of his head, he'll come.

*The three leave. Much bowing low.*

WANG: When the old whisky has been drunk, maybe the new whisky will be drunk.

*JIP bangs on the box.*

(*To the* VISITORS:) The god who is knocking on the boards of the prayer box wants five rupees. Divine grace is being showered on you. Sexton, take up the collection.

# 6

## WIDOW BEGBICK'S CANTEEN

*Late at night.* GALY GAY *is seated on a wooden chair, sleeping.* POLLY, URIAH, *and* JESSE *appear at the window.*

POLLY: Still sitting there. Looks like an Irish squirrel, huh?

URIAH: Maybe he didn't want to leave because it was raining.

JESSE: Hard to tell, but now we're going to need him again.

POLLY: You don't think Jip's coming back?

JESSE: Polly, I know Jip's not coming back.

POLLY: We can hardly tell this porter that again.

JESSE: What do you think, Uriah?

URIAH: I think I'll hit the hay.

POLLY: But if this porter gets up and goes through that door, our heads will be hanging by a hair.

JESSE: True. But I'm going to sleep too. You can't ask too much of a man.

POLLY: Maybe it's all to the good if we do hit the hay. It's depressing! And all the rain's fault, too.

*The three leave.*

# 7

# INSIDE THE PAGODA OF THE YELLOW MONKS

*Projection:* SEE WITH YOUR OWN EYES THE QUAINT AND INTRIGUING RITUALS OF INDIAN RELIGION BUT DO NOT OVERLOOK THE COLLECTION PLATE FOR, AS CONFUCIUS SAYS, EVEN A GOD MUST EAT.

*Toward morning. Large posters everywhere. Sound of an old phonograph and a drum. In the background rather largescale religious ceremonies seem to be taking place.*

WANG (*to the* SEXTON): Roll those camel-dung balls faster, you piece of manure. (*At the box:*) Still asleep, Mister Soldier?

JIP'S VOICE: Do we get out soon, Jesse? This carriage rocks terribly! It's as narrow as a latrine.

WANG: Now don't imagine you're in a railway carriage, Mister Soldier. It's only the whiskey in your honorable head that shakes.

JIP: Hey! Who is it?

WANG (*in the voice of a fat rat*): This moderately fat rat is your friend Wang from Tientsin, Colonel.

JIP: The city I'm in—what's it like?

WANG: A miserable one, honored patron, a hole named Kilkoa.

JIP: Let me out!

WANG (*toward the rear*): When you have rolled the camel dung into balls, lay out the balls on a bowl, beat the drum, and light them.

JIP *knocks loudly.*

Stop! Believers all, stop! Remain where you are one minute! The god is speaking to you—in claps of

148

thunder. Count the claps carefully! One, two, three, four. No, five. Too bad: once again it is five rupees you are to sacrifice to him. (*Knocks at the prayer box. In a kind voice:*) Here's a steak, Mister Soldier, to feed your honorable face. (WANG *lets him out.*)

JIP: How did I get here?

WANG: Through the air, Mister General, you got in through the air.

JIP: Where was I when you found me?

WANG: Deigning to rest your limbs in an old palanquin, sublime one.

JIP: And where are my comrades?

WANG: Beyond the Punjab Mountains. They left last month. But here's your steak.

JIP: What? How about me? Where was I? What was I doing while they marched off?

WANG: Whisky, much whisky, one thousand bottles. You earned some money too.

JIP: Didn't any of them ask for me?

WANG: Alas, no.

JIP: That's very disagreeable.

WANG: If they should come now—looking for a man in a white soldier's uniform—shall I bring them to see you, Mister Minister of War?

JIP: You needn't bother.

WANG: If you don't wish to be disturbed, Johnny, just step inside this box, Johnny, when people turn up who offend your honorable eye.

JIP: Where's that steak? (*Sits and eats.*) It's too small! What's that terrible noise?

*Drumming. Smoke from the camel-dung balls rises toward the ceiling.*

WANG: It's the prayers of the faithful, they're on their knees over there.

JIP: Who're they praying to?

WANG: That is their secret.

JIP: This is good steak, but I have no right to be sitting here. Polly and Jesse must certainly have waited for me. Maybe they're still waiting. It tastes like butter. It's bad of me to be eating it.

WANG (*who flits about* JIP *dusting off his clothes, and gradually changing his posture to that of a Buddha*): Mister General!

JIP: Polly's just saying to Jesse: Jip will turn up, when he's sober Jip will turn up.

WANG: Mister Minister of War!

JIP: Maybe Uriah won't wait so manfully because of course Uriah is a bad man. But Jesse and Polly will say: Jip'll turn up. There can be little doubt this is a suitable meal for me after all that drink.

WANG: Mister Honored Patron!

JIP: If only Jesse didn't rely so implicitly on good old Jip. But he'll surely be saying: Jip won't betray us. Naturally, that's hard for me to bear.

WANG: Mister Sublime One!

JIP: It's all wrong for me to be sitting here. But the meat is good meat.

WANG: Mister Celestial Deity! (WANG *places a crown on* JIP's *head.*)

*Enter* BEGBICK, *who sings:*

## Song of the Ganges River

Now I like to read of a doughty deed
Performed by a doughty hero
In a book that proclaims such immortal names
As Genghis Khan and Nero.
And I like to recite the tale of a fight
(Specially a fight that we won)
But though I may sing of a conquering king
I have no desire to be one:
  Take a look at the Ganges River
  As it sweeps from Benares to the sea!
  Could I swim against that current? Never!
  Who'd even make a stab at it? Not me.
  Why should I help King George commit his
               crimes?
  I prefer to read about them in the *Times*.

# 8

## WIDOW BEGBICK'S CANTEEN

*Projection:* WE DON'T WANT TO FIGHT
BUT BY JINGO IF WE DO
WE'VE GOT THE SHIPS
WE'VE GOT THE MEN
WE'VE GOT THE MONEY TOO.
—*Gautama Buddha*

*Early morning.* GALY DAY *is asleep on a wooden chair. The three are playing billiards.*

POLLY: Jip will turn up.

JESSE: Jip won't betray us.

POLLY: When he's sober, Jip will turn up.

URIAH: Hard to tell. Anyhow, we won't let this porter go, with Jip still walking the tiles.

JESSE: He didn't leave.

POLLY: He must be frozen. Spent the night on the chair.

URIAH: Anyhow, we got a good night's sleep. Now we're on the up and up again.

POLLY: And Jip will turn up. With the good sense of a well-rested soldier I see it quite clearly. That yellow bullfrog took advantage of our tiredness. When Jip's whisky is done, Jip will turn up.

*Enter* MISTER WANG. *Goes to the bar and rings.* BEGBICK *comes in.*

BEGBICK: No liquor for native stinkers! Not even yellow ones!

WANG: For a white one: seven bottles of good old Victoria whisky.

BEGBICK: Seven bottles for a white man? (*She gives him seven bottles.*)

WANG: For a white one, yes. (*Bows to the four and leaves.*)

JESSE, POLLY *and* URIAH *look at each other.*

URIAH: Seven bottles of Victoria whisky? Now Jip will NOT turn up. And therefore this Galy Gay of Kilkoa must become Jeraiah Jip of Tipperary.

*The three look the sleeping* GALY GAY *over.*

POLLY: How can we get away with it, Uriah? We have nothing but Jip's papers.

JESSE: They're enough. There's got to be a new Jip. Why all the fuss about people? One's as good as none at all. It's impossible to speak of less than two hundred at a time.

POLLY: But what will he say when we turn him into a soldier?

JESSE: A man like that does the turning all on his own. Throw him into a puddle and he'll grow webs between his fingers in two days.

URIAH: Whatever happens to him, we've got to have a fourth man. Wake him up!

POLLY (*wakes* GALY GAY *up*): A lucky thing you didn't go away, dear sir. Circumstances have arisen to prevent our comrade Jip from making a punctual appearance.

URIAH: You are of Irish descent?

GALY GAY: I wouldn't be surprised.

URIAH: That's a distinct advantage. Mister Galy Gay, you're not more than forty, I trust?

GALY GAY: No. Less.

URIAH: Splendid! Don't tell me you have flat feet?

GALY GAY: Somewhat.

URIAH: That decides it. Your happiness is assured. For the time being, you may stay.

GALY GAY: I'm afraid my wife's waiting for me. Because of a fish.

POLLY: We understand and respect your solicitude. It's worthy of an Irishman. But your presence here is very welcome. What's more, it fits. The opportunity is perhaps at hand for you to become a soldier.

GALY GAY *is silent.*

A soldier's life is pleasant. Every week we receive a handful of money exclusively for tramping up and down India and keeping an eye on these streets and pagodas. Observe those comfortable woolen blankets, they are delivered free to every soldier. Take a look at this gun which bears the stamp of the firm Everett and Co. Most of the time we amuse ourselves fishing. And Mamma—as we have christened the army in jest—Mamma buys the fishing tackle. As we fish, several military bands play one after the other. You spend the rest of the day smoking in your bungalow or lazily observing the golden palace of some Rajah, whom moreover, you may shoot, should it take your fancy. The ladies expect many things of us soldiers, but never money. As you will admit, this is a further convenience.

GALY GAY: A soldier's life *is* pleasant.

URIAH: So without more ado you can hold on to that nice uniform, and at all times be addressed as Mister. Mister Jip.

GALY GAY: You wouldn't make a poor porter unhappy?

URIAH: You want to leave?

GALY GAY: Yes, I must be leaving.

JESSE: Polly, give him his clothes.

POLLY (*with his clothes*): Why don't you want to be Jip, actually?

BLOODY FIVE *pops up in the window.*

GALY GAY: Because I'm Galy Gay. (*Goes to the door. The three look at each other.*)

URIAH: Wait just a minute.

POLLY: Maybe you know the saying: Make haste slowly.

URIAH: You're dealing with men who do not lightly incur obligations to strangers.

JESSE: Whatever your name might be, you should certainly be rewarded for your kindness.

URIAH: It's a matter of—yes, just stay there a minute—a deal.

GALY GAY *stays there.*

JESSE: The best deal that Kilkoa has to offer, isn't it, Polly?

URIAH: And it is our duty to offer you a chance to participate in this really tremendous deal.

GALY GAY: Did you say deal?

URIAH: Maybe I did. But then you have no time.

GALY GAY: There's time and time.

POLLY: Ah so you might have time. If you knew about this deal, you would have time. Lord Kitchener had time to conquer Egypt.

GALY GAY: Is it a big deal?

POLLY: Maybe it would be—for the Maharajah of Peshawar. For such a great man as yourself, maybe it wouldn't be.

GALY GAY: I can always turn around and go home. (*He sits.*)

BLOODY FIVE *disappears from the window.*

POLLY: What an elephant!

GALY GAY (*overhearing him*): An elephant? Of course, an elephant would be a gold mine.

URIAH: Elephant?! And how we have an elephant!

GALY GAY: On hand? I mean: is this elephant on hand?

POLLY: An elephant! How he insists on an elephant!

GALY GAY: Do you have your elephant on hand?

POLLY: Was a deal ever made with an elephant which was not on hand?

GALY GAY: Good. If that's settled, I'd just like to carve out my own piece of meat, Mister Polly.

URIAH (*hesitating*): But . . . don't overlook the character of the enemy.

155

GALY GAY: The enemy?

POLLY: The human typhoon.

JESSE: The tiger of Kilkoa.

URIAH: Sergeant Bloody Five.

GALY GAY: What's he done to get a name like that?

POLLY: Oh nothing. Once in a while he takes someone who gives the wrong name at roll call, wraps him in six square feet of canvas, and rolls him under the feet of his elephants.

GALY GAY: So you'd need a man with a head on his shoulders.

URIAH: Comrade, you have a big head.

POLLY: There must be something in it—a big head like that.

GALY GAY: Don't mention it. Though I do know a riddle that might interest cultured gentlemen such as you.

JESSE: You see before you three powerful solvers of riddles.

GALY GAY: It goes this way. White, a mammal; sees behind as good as in front.

JESSE: It's very difficult.

GALY GAY: You won't get anywhere with this riddle. I myself didn't get anywhere with this riddle. A mammal; white; sees behind as good as in front. A blind white horse.

URIAH: That riddle is terrific.

POLLY: And you carry all this in your head?

GALY GAY: Mostly, because I don't write very well. But for almost any deal, I'm the man.

BLOODY FIVE (enters): One small moment. There's a woman outside looking for a man named Galy Gray.

GALY GAY: Galy Gay! He's called Galy Gay, the chap she's looking for!

BLOODY FIVE: Step inside, Mrs. Gray, here's someone that knows your husband.

URIAH *lets out a frightful oath. The three quickly go and stand against the wall.*

156

GALY GAY: Leave it all to me. Galy Gay has tasted blood.

BLOODY FIVE, *humming "Pack your kit bag, Johnny," re-enters with* MRS. GAY.

MRS. GAY: Excuse a humble woman, good sirs, also her dress, I was in such a hurry. Ah, so there you are, Galy Gay! But can it really be you—in uniform!

GALY GAY: No.

MRS. GAY: I don't understand. How come you're in a uniform? You look good in it too. You are a very peculiar man, Galy Gay.

URIAH: Her brain's affected.

MRS. GAY: It isn't easy to have a husband who can't say no. Lithe as a squirrel he may be but his heart's as soft as a raw egg.

URIAH: I'd like to know who she's talking to. These are insults.

BLOODY FIVE: Please go on, Mrs. Gray. Your voice is sweeter than sweet music to me.

MRS. GAY: I don't know what you're after this time with your famous self-conceit. But you'll come to a bad end. Now come along with me. But say something. Has your voice gone?

GALY GAY: You're confusing me with someone else. And what you're saying about him is stupid and not right.

MRS. GAY: What do you say? Confusing? Have you been drinking? He can't hold his liquor, you know.

GALY GAY: I'm as much your Galy Gay as I am Commandant of this camp. . . .

MRS. GAY: It was just this time yesterday that I put the water in the pot. But you never brought the fish.

GALY GAY: And what sort of fish would that be now?

BLOODY FIVE: A remarkable case. Such terrible thoughts come flooding into my mind! Do you know this woman?

157

*The three shake their heads.*

What about you?

GALY GAY: In my lifetime, between Ireland and Kilkoa, I have seen much. But I never set eyes on this woman before.

BLOODY FIVE: Tell the lady what your name is.

GALY GAY: Jeraiah Jip.

MRS. GAY: This is outrageous. Though when I look at him, Sergeant, it's almost as if he was not Galy Gay the porter but something different, I couldn't exactly say what.

BLOODY FIVE: Well, we shall see!

*Bewildered,* MRS. GAY *leaves with* BLOODY FIVE.

GALY GAY (*singing*):

Let's go to Benares
Where the sun is shining!

It's always been said of the Galy Gays: they sure hit the nail on the head.

URIAH (*to* POLLY): Before the sun has set seven more times, this man must be another man.

POLLY: But will it work, Uriah? Turning a man into another man?

URIAH: Yes. One man's as good as another.

POLLY: But the army might break camp any minute. Listen!

*Trumpets sound breaking of camp. Drums.*

BLOODY FIVE (*entering*): The war which was planned has now broken out. Everyone on the trains with all elephants and cannon! We are setting out for the icebound frontier of ancient Tibet. (*Exit humming "Pack your kit bag, Johnny."*)

GALY GAY *takes his bundle of clothes and tries to slip out. The three seize him and throw him onto a chair.*

158

*Enter* MASTER OF CEREMONIES.

MASTER OF CEREMONIES: This evening's entertainment is brought to you by His Majesty's Imperial Indian Army. All proceeds to His Majesty's Recruiting Campaign. And now, to bring the first half of our show to a fitting close, Sergeant Solly Schmitt with special army quartet will sing our theme song: "*A Man's A Man.*" Solly!

*Enter* SOLLY SCHMITT *and* QUARTET.

### A Man's A Man

So you're in the army as well, Danny boy?
For I'm in the army as well, Danny boy!
And when I see old pals like you
I'm glad I'm in the army too.
Had you never seen me here before?
I had never seen you here before!
That's all right, Dan,
For a man is a man.
You needn't shout:
Really, Dan, my dear man,
What is there to shout about?
For men are men.
Let us say that again:
A man's a man.
So it's all right, Dan.
Kilkoa's sun shines down upon
Six thousand soldiers and their doom.
(When they are dead no tears are shed.
None on the list is ever missed.)
And so we sing: who cares on whom
The ruddy sun of old Kilkoa shone?

# INTERJECTION: BEGBICK ON BRECHT

**WIDOW LEOCADIA BEGBICK:**

A man's a man is Mister Brecht's contention.
But that is something anyone might mention.
Mr. Brecht appends this item to the bill:
You can do with a human being what you will.
Take him apart like a car, rebuild him bit by bit—
As you will see, he has nothing to lose by it.
We come to this chap—like one man to another—
And with emphasis, but no fuss, persuade our
                            brother
To adjust to this world as it is and let rot
The fish he planned to boil in his private pot.
You now will see the ground beneath your feet
Melt away like sleet
And please don't miss the moral of the case:
That this world is a dangerous place.

# 9

## WIDOW BEGBICK'S CANTEEN

*Projection:* THREE MORE METAMORPHOSES! *First:* A CIVIL-
IAN TURNS INTO A SOLDIER. *Second:* A SOLDIER TURNS
INTO A CIVILIAN. *Third:* A CANTEEN TURNS INTO EMPTY
SPACE. THIS VERY BIG NUMBER IS DIVIDED INTO SIX LITTLE
NUMBERS.

*Noise of a camp breaking up.* GALY GAY *still there with*
URIAH, POLLY, *and* JESSE.

BEGBICK (*runs through the canteen, driving her* DAUGHTERS
*before her*): The army's pulling out. If no one gives
us a hand, we'll be stuck here, with all the King's
men off in old Tibet. (*Exit with* DAUGHTERS.)

*The three eye each other.*

URIAH (*to* GALY GAY): Step outside a moment, would you?
JESSE: We'll be sending for that elephant.

*Exit* GALY GAY.

POLLY: Now he'll have to be reconstructed on the double.
URIAH: For which we need an elephant. For if this Galy
Gay makes a deal with an elephant, and there's
something wrong about this deal, he will prefer
being Jeraiah Jip the Soldier to being Galy Gay the
Crook.
POLLY: So the important thing is for us to make an
elephant.
URIAH: Jesse, stick this pole in the elephant's head from
the wall there, and Polly, you take a whisky bottle,
and I'll spread this map over you both.

*They build an artificial elephant.*

BEGBICK: What are you doing with my elephant's head?

POLLY: Making an elephant. And if you care to help us, we'll pack your canteen for you.

BEGBICK: What do you want me to do?

JESSE: When Galy Gay comes in, tell him you're in the market for an elephant.

BEGBICK: Good. And you gunners will pack my canteen.

JOBIA: Here are your soldiers, mamma, the finest flower of His Majesty's Army.

SOLDIERS *have come on; they watch the three, who are building a small elephant around* JESSE *and* POLLY.

SOLDIER: What's all this about your fourth man?

JESSE: Our fourth man, Jeraiah Jip, has a touch of sunstroke and thinks he's—

URIAH: —a porter from foreign parts. Name of Galy Gay.

POLLY: So we think we are—

JESSE: An army elephant, name of Billy Humph.

GALY GAY (*at the window*): Is the elephant here yet?

POLLY: Almost. Give us one more minute.

URIAH: Polly, take the whisky bottle, so the elephant can make water and, when Galy Gay's looking, pour away. (*To the* SOLDIERS:) Listen. We're going to make him a present of the elephant and tell him to sell it. Then when he sells it, we arrest him.

SOLDIER: D'you think he'll take that for an elephant?

POLLY: Is it such a bad job?

URIAH (*angry*): He *will* take that for an elephant. Because he's interested in buying and selling. I tell you he'd take this whisky bottle for an elephant if someone pointed at it and said: sell me that elephant.

SOLDIER: We don't believe you.

URIAH (*looking out the window*): Come in, Mister Galy Gay. The deal is in full swing.

GALY GAY (*enters*): And what's it all about?

URIAH: This deal concerns the surplus and non-registered army elephant Billy Humph. Our battle cry is: to each his elephant.

GALY GAY: Very enlightening. Who's auctioning him off?

URIAH: Anyone who can sign his name as the owner.

GALY GAY: But who *is* going to sign his name as the owner?

URIAH: Would *you* like to?

GALY GAY: Yes. But then my name must be kept out of it.

URIAH: Care for a cigar?

GALY GAY: Why?

URIAH: So you can preserve your equanimity. The elephant has a bit of a cold.

GALY GAY: Do we have a buyer?

BEGBICK (*goes to* GALY GAY): Oh, Mr. Galy Gay! I want an elephant. Do you happen to have one? It isn't important if it's large or small. But I've wanted an elephant ever since I was a child.

GALY GAY: Widow Begbick, it is possible I have just the one for you.

BEGBICK: Take the walls away. That one first. The cannon will be coming by any moment.

SOLDIER: Right you are, Widow Begbick.

BEGBICK: Hey! come out and make music, so the soldiers can dismantle our canteen and like it.

*The three* DAUGHTERS *come and play.*

URIAH: And while you're all at it, I'll be thinking what to do with him. (*He sits down on a rocking chair.*)

*During the singing of the first strophe of the song "A Man's A Man" by the* SOLDIERS, *one wall of the canteen is taken down. The elephant can now be dimly seen.*

### A Man's A Man

So you're in the army as well, Danny boy!

For I'm in the army as well, Danny boy!
And when I see old pals like you
I'm glad I'm in the army too!
Had you never seen me here before?
I had never seen you here before!
That's all right, Dan.
For a man is a man.
You needn't shout.
Really, Dan, my dear man,
What is there to shout about?

*First Number*

URIAH (*whistles*): First Number: the Elephant Deal. The machine-gun unit which has been called The Scum hands over an elephant to the man who wishes to have his name kept out of it. (*He leads the elephant forward by a rope.*) Billy Humph, Champion of Bengal, Elephant in the service of the British Army, etcetera!

GALY GAY (*catches sight of the elephant and is terrified*): Is that the army elephant?

SOLDIER: He has a bad cold, as you can see from his blanket.

*The elephant urinates.*

GALY GAY: The blanket isn't the worst of it. (*He walks around in some consternation.*)

BEGBICK: I'm in the market for that elephant. When I was a child I wanted an elephant as big as the Hindu Kush Range, but now that one will do.

GALY GAY: Well, Widow Begbick, if you really want this elephant, I'm its owner.

BLOODY FIVE (*off*): "Pack your kit bag, Johnny!"

SOLDIER: The Tiger of Kilkoa!

*They seem to flee.*

164

BEGBICK: Everyone stay here. I won't have my elephant taken away from me. (*Exit.*)

URIAH (*to* GALY GAY): You hold the elephant for a minute.

GALY GAY, *alone, holds the elephant by the very end of the rope.*

SOLDIERS *watch over him from behind a wall.*

SOLDIER: Now really!

SECOND SOLDIER: He doesn't dare look at it.

THIRD SOLDIER: He holds it as far away from him as he can.

GALY GAY: My mother used to tell me one knows nothing for certain. But you, Galy Gay, you know nothing, either for certain or otherwise. You went out this morning to purchase a fish; you now have an elephant; and who knows what tomorrow may bring? But it's all one so long as you get paid.

SOLDIER (*at back*): Has he gone?

URIAH (*ditto*): The Tiger of Kilkoa was only passing by. Widow Begbick gave him a good hard look.

*Second Number*

URIAH: Now comes the Second Number: The elephant at auction. The man who wants his name kept out of it sells the elephant.

SOLDIERS *come in.*

SOLDIER: You still have your doubts about this elephant?

GALY GAY: Now he's being bought, I have no doubts.

URIAH: Of course not. If he's being bought, he's all right, huh?

GALY GAY: I can't say no to that. An elephant's an elephant, especially when bought.

URIAH: And here comes Widow Begbick with the check.

BEGBICK: Does the elephant belong to you?

GALY GAY: Like my own foot. (*He stands near the elephant.*) Weighs three hundredweight. And when it comes to chopping wood, a whole forest is no more to him than a blade of grass in the wind. Billy Humph is worth a small fortune.

BEGBICK: Three hundred rupees.

GALY GAY: Three hundred rupees! Going, going, gone, Widow Begbick, you may now take over Billy Humph from his former owner, and pay for him with a check.

BEGBICK: Your name?

GALY GAY: I want my name kept out of it.

BEGBICK: Now give me a pencil so I can make out the check—to the man who wants his name kept out of it.

URIAH (*aside to others*): When he takes the check, grab him.

BEGBICK (*with a roar of laughter*): Here it is, O man who wants his name kept out of it! Your check!

SOLDIER (*lays a hand on his shoulder*): In the King's name, what are you up to?

GALY GAY: Me? Nothing. (*He laughs foolishly.*)

SOLDIER: What elephant is this?

GALY GAY: Which elephant is that?

SOLDIER: Chiefly the one behind you. And don't try to get out of it, see!

GALY GAY: I don't know the elephant.

SOLDIERS: Oho! We can testify this man said the elephant was his.

BEGBICK: Like his own foot, he said.

GALY GAY (*tries to leave*): I'm afraid I must go home. My wife is waiting, it's urgent. I'll come back and talk it over later. Goodbye. (*To* BILLY *who follows hard on his heels:*) Billy! Stay there, Billy, don't be so willful! Your sugar cane grows *there*!

URIAH: Stop! (*To the men:*) Take your pistols. Cover this crook.

POLLY, *inside* BILLY HUMPH, *laughs loudly.* URIAH *hits him.*

Polly, shut your trap.

*The map slides down.* POLLY *is now visible.*

POLLY: Damn!

GALY GAY, *now completely confused, looks at* POLLY, *then from one to the other. The elephant runs off.*

BEGBICK (*walks over to* GALY GAY): What's this? (*Pointing toward Billy*:) That isn't an elephant at all. It's a map and some men. All fake! A fake elephant for my real gold!

SOLDIER: Arrest him!

SECOND SOLDIER: Galy Gay the Crook, arrest him!

URIAH *ties up* GALY GAY.

BLOODY FIVE (*stands in the doorway*): "Pack your kit bag, Johnny!"

BEGBICK (*puts a cloth over* GALY GAY's *head*): How are you Sergeant? (*To the* SOLDIERS:) Pack up the canteen and sing!

BLOODY FIVE: What's that you're covering up with a cloth?

BEGBICK: Oh nothing. (*Roaring, to the* SOLDIERS:) Sing!

*The canteen is further dismantled during the singing of the second strophe of "A Man's A Man."* URIAH *sits thinking in his rocking chair.*

### A Man's A Man 2

So, Dan, you had rice for your dinner today?
For, Dan, I had rice for my dinner today!
Without a chicken in the pot
A soldier's life is not so hot.
And, Dan, after dinner did you throw up?
After dinner, Dan, I too threw up!

167

That's all right, Dan.
For a man is a man.
You needn't shout.
Really, Dan my dear man,
What is there to shout about?

BLOODY FIVE: What's that you were covering up?

BEGBICK: Are you making trouble in my canteen? Fingers to your trouser seams when you speak to me, you old snot-nose! Never enter my canteen again in that uniform!

BLOODY FIVE: What?

BEGBICK: If you come to Widow Begbick's Bar, you will wear tails and a bowler hat!

BLOODY FIVE: Today, Bloody Five, your blood is again as stormy as the Ganges. You can never survive this rainy night without the daughters of the old cloaca. Widow Begbick, I must see your daughters.

BEGBICK: Sergeant Fairchild, I must see your bowler hat.

BLOODY FIVE: Never, never, never, never, never, (*As he goes:*) If you do this, Bloody Five, you'll have given in to the sensual side of your nature, hook, line, and sinker. (*Exit.*)

## Third Number

URIAH (*whistles. The* SOLDIERS *uncover* GALY GAY): Right. Now comes the Third Number: the trial of the man who wants his name kept out of it. Make a circle around the crook, cross-examine him, and don't stop till you know the naked truth.

GALY GAY: I beg leave to say something.

URIAH: You've said plenty. Who knows what the man was called who put the elephant on sale?

SOLDIER: He was called Galy Gay.

URIAH: Who can testify to that?

SOLDIERS: We can.

URIAH: What does the accused have to say about it?

GALY GAY: It was someone who wanted his name kept out of it.

SOLDIERS *murmur*.

SOLDIER: I heard him say he was Galy Gay.

URIAH: Aren't you?

GALY GAY (*slyly*): Well, if I were Galy Gay, maybe I'd be the man you're looking for.

URIAH: So you are not Galy Gay.

GALY GAY (*in a whisper*): No. I am not.

URIAH: And you were not present maybe when Billy Humph was put on auction?

GALY GAY: No. I wasn't present.

URIAH: But you saw that it was someone called Galy Gay who made the sale?

GALY GAY: (*lifting his hand as witness, just as the* SOLDIERS *had done*): Yes. I can testify to that.

URIAH: Then you will have it that you *were* there?

GALY GAY: I can testify to that.

URIAH: Did you all hear? Do you all see the moon? The moon is high in the sky, and he is deep in this dirty elephant deal. In the Billy Humph business, he wasn't altogether straightforward.

SOLDIER: No.

SECOND SOLDIER: He certainly was not.

SOLDIER: The fellow said it was an elephant. But it wasn't.

SECOND SOLDIER: It was made of paper.

URIAH: Then he sold a fake elephant. That would mean the death penalty, of course. What do you say to that?

GALY GAY: At first, it was a regular elephant, later it was a fake, and it's very hard to sort everything out, High Court of Justice.

URIAH: It's certainly quite involved, but even so I think you'll have to be shot, you've brought yourself under such grave suspicion. Now listen, I've heard of a

169

soldier, who was called Jip, and admitted it at various roll calls, and he wanted people to believe he was Galy Gay. Are you this Jip maybe?

GALY GAY: No. Certainly not.

URIAH: So you're not called Jip? What *are* you called?

GALY GAY *is silent*.

No answer? Then you are someone who wants his name kept out of it?

GALY GAY *is silent*.

Are you the man, maybe, who wanted his name kept out of it when the elephant was sold? Silent again? That is tremendously suspicious, almost enough to convict you. Well, now we must confer.

*They confer*.

URIAH: He's willing not to be Galy Gay now, but I think we'll need to threaten him with the death penalty a little more before he'll be Jeraiah Jip.

GALY GAY: Can you hear what they are saying?

SOLDIERS: No.

GALY GAY: Are they saying I am this Galy Gay?

SOLDIER: They're saying it's no longer certain.

GALY GAY: Yes, it's no longer certain, is it?

BEGBICK (*enters; to* GALY GAY): Note this, pal: one man is no man. (*Exit*.)

JESSE (*enters*): Isn't that Galy Gay sitting there all tied up?

SOLDIERS: Hey, you! Answer!

GALY GAY: I think you're confusing me with someone else, Jesse. Take a closer look.

JESSE: Oh, then you're not Galy Gay?

GALY GAY *shakes his head*.

Go away for a minute. I have to talk to him: he's just been sentenced to death.

GALY GAY: Has it gone that far? Oh Jesse, help me. You are a great soldier.

170

JESSE: How did it all come about?

GALY GAY: I don't know. We were smoking and drinking, and I jabbered my soul away.

JESSE: They're saying one Galy Gay is going to be killed.

GALY GAY: That can't be me.

JESSE: So you're not Galy Gay? Look me in the eye. I'm Jesse, your friend. Aren't you Galy Gay from Kilkoa?

GALY GAY: No.

JESSE: There were four of us when we left Kankerdan. Were you there?

GALY GAY: Yes.

JESSE: I agree.

URIAH (*back with the* SOLDIERS; *to* GALY GAY): Stand up, man without a name, and give ear. The military court of Kilkoa has condemned you to be shot by eight riflemen.

GALY GAY: That cannot happen.

URIAH: It *is* happening. And pay attention, pal, because, firstly, you stole and sold an army elephant, which is larceny, because secondly, you sold an elephant which was not an elephant, which is fraud, and because, thirdly, you have neither a name nor an identity card and may be a spy or even a swindler who gave the wrong name at roll call.

GALY GAY: Oh, Uriah, why do you take this tone to me?

URIAH: Now come. Handle yourself like a soldier. March!

SOLDIER: Go with him and be shot.

GALY GAY (*throws himself on the ground*): I'm not the man you're looking for. I don't even know him. My name is Jip, I swear it. What is an elephant compared to a man? And I don't even know the creature. I didn't see the elephant. Only the rope I was holding. Please go away! I'm someone else. At most I bear that man some slight resemblance, and you confuse me with him. I am not Galy Gay. I am not.

SOLDIER: Yes, you are.

SECOND SOLDIER: And no one else is.

THIRD SOLDIER: Under Kilkoa's three rubber trees, Galy Gay will see his blood flow.

FOURTH SOLDIER: Come on!

GALY GAY: Oh, dear, surely there must be formalities, the charges must be written up, and it'll be found that it wasn't me, and I'm not called Galy Gay? A considered judgment must be arrived at. You don't do such a job between noon and midday, when a man's to be sent to the slaughter!

SOLDIERS: March!

GALY GAY: What do you mean, march? I am not your man. I wanted to buy a fish, are there any fish here? What are those cannon rolling in the distance? What's that battle music roaring outside? I'm not going to budge. I'll hold on to this grass, yes even if it's fake. This must all stop, I insist! But why is no one here? Uriah, Jesse, Polly, help me!

URIAH (to BEGBICK): The moon is up, all the way up, and at last he consents to be Jip. I'm glad the cannon haven't gone by yet.

*The cannon are heard rolling past.*

BEGBICK: The cannon! We must be on that train. Get all the canteen things together!

SOLDIER: At your service, Widow Begbick.

URIAH *sits in his chair. The canteen is being further dismantled during the singing of the third strophe of "A Man's A Man."*

### A Man's A Man 3

You saw Jenny Smith as well, Danny boy?
I saw Jenny Smith as well, Danny boy!
And Jenny Smith, that dear old hen,
Makes army life look good again!
And Dan, did you sleep with Miss Smith as well?
Danny boy, I slept with Miss Smith as well!

172

That's all right, Dan.
For a man is a man.
You needn't shout.
Really, Dan my dear man,
What is there to shout about?

## Fourth Number

URIAH (*whistles*): Now comes the Fourth Number: the shooting of Galy Gay in the army barracks at Kilkoa.

BEGBICK: When they load the elephant and you're not finished, that'll be the end of your story, my men!

GALY GAY *is led back and then forward again. He walks like the protagonist of a tragedy.*

Room there for a felon condemned to death by the military tribunal!

SOLDIER: Look, a man's going to be shot.

SECOND SOLDIER: That may be a pity, he isn't very old.

THIRD SOLDIER: He doesn't even know how he got into this.

URIAH: Halt! Would you like to relieve yourself for the last time?

GALY GAY: Yes.

URIAH: Guard him.

GALY GAY: I heard someone say the soldiers must leave when the elephants arrive so I've got to be slow.

SOLDIER: You've got to be quick.

GALY GAY: I can't. Is that the moon?

SECOND SOLDIER: Yes, it's getting late.

GALY GAY: Isn't that Widow Begbick's Bar where we always used to drink?

URIAH: No, buddy, it's the rifle range, and that's the Johnny-are-your-pants-dry-wall. Hey! Stand in line there, and load those guns. There should be eight of them.

SOLDIER: The light's bad.

SECOND SOLDIER: You can hardly see.

URIAH: Yes, the light's bad.

GALY GAY: Listen, this will never do. When you shoot, you've got to be able to see.

URIAH (*blindfolds* GALY GAY. *Loudly*): Load all guns! (*Quietly:*) What are you doing there, Polly? You're *really* putting a bullet in! Take that bullet out!

POLLY: Oh, excuse me. I almost *really* loaded my gun. We nearly had a *real* misfortune on our hands!

*The elephants are heard passing at the back. Everyone stands for a moment petrified.*

BEGBICK: The elephants!

URIAH: All that makes no difference. He must be shot. I'm going to count up to three. One!

GALY GAY: That will be enough, Uriah. The elephants have arrived, haven't they? Am I to stay on now, Uriah? Why are you all so terribly quiet?

URIAH: Two!

GALY GAY (*laughs*): You're funny, Uriah. I can't see you but your voice sounds dead serious.

URIAH: And one more makes—

GALY GAY: Stop! Don't say three, or you'll be sorry. If you shoot now, you'll hit me. Listen! I confess. I confess I don't know what happened to me. Believe me, I'm a man—now don't laugh—who doesn't know who he is. But I'm Galy Gay, that I do know. The man that's to be shot, I'm not him. But who am I? I've forgotten. Last night, when it was raining, I knew. But was it raining last night? And when you look toward the spot where this voice comes from, over here or over there, that's me. Say to that spot: "Galy Gay" or something. Say "Have pity." Say: "Give me a piece of meat." The place where it disappears is Galy Gay, also the place where it pops up again. Remember this at least: when you find someone who's forgotten who he is, that's me. Please let him go—please—one more time.

URIAH *has said something in* POLLY's *ear. Now* POLLY *runs behind* GALY GAY *and flourishes a great big club.*

URIAH: "One more time" equals "no more time." Three!

GALY GAY *lets out a shriek.*

Fire!!

GALY GAY *falls in a faint.*

POLLY: Halt!
URIAH (*shouts*): Shoot! So he'll hear he's dead!

*They shoot.*

Throw him over there. He fell all by himself!
VOICE OF BLOODY FIVE: "Pack your kit bag, Johnny!"
BEGBICK: Pack up! Pack up!
BLOODY FIVE (*enters in tails and bowler hat*): Who's shooting around here? Everybody stand still!
URIAH (*smashes his hat down on his head from behind*): Shut your mouth, civilian!

*A burst of laughter.*

BEGBICK: Pack up! Pack up! (*She takes* BLOODY FIVE *over to her* DAUGHTERS *who are making music.*)

*The canteen is further dismantled during the singing of the fourth strophe of "A Man's A Man."*

### A Man's A Man 4

So, Dan, are you packing your kit bag as well?
For, Dan, I am packing my kit bag as well!
And when I see you pack and go
My soldier's breast is full of woe!
But, Dan, have you nothing to put in your bag?
I have nothing, either to put in my bag!
    That's all right, Dan.
    For a man is a man.

You needn't shout!
Really, Dan, my dear man,
What is there to shout about?

## Fifth Number

URIAH (*whistles*): Well, then, a certain Bloody Gent who insists on sticking his nose into everything must be razed to the ground. This Number—the Fifth—is a slight digression.

BEGBICK: It's nearly eleven o'clock. Soon now you'll hear the train whistle!

URIAH, POLLY, JESSE, BEGBICK, BLOODY FIVE, *and the three* DAUGHTERS *sit around a table*.

BLOODY FIVE: First of all, ladies, it is my intention to lay before you a few items from my photographic collection. Rarities in their way. I have certain items that even the British Museum hasn't got.

BEGBICK: If they can drink your health in several glasses of liquor, they'll enjoy looking at your photographs, Mister Fairchild.

BLOODY FIVE: Look, Widow, she's on her third glass already. (*Pointing to* GALY GAY:) Who's that drunk? Lying there like a corpse?

URIAH: Why don't you show us you can shoot, my dear Fairchild?

BEGBICK: Hardly one woman in ten can resist such a sharpshooter as the sergeant!

BLOODY FIVE: No!

SOLDIER: Oh, go on.

SECOND SOLDIER: Shoot, Bloody Five.

BLOODY FIVE: Will you put the lights out if I do?

*They laugh.*

JOBIA: Oh, Bloody, do it for my sake, you really should. I'll put out the lights, too, whenever you wish.

176

BLOODY FIVE: I place an egg here. How many paces?

SOLDIER: Four.

BLOODY FIVE (*goes to a considerable distance*): I take a plain ordinary army pistol. (*He shoots.*)

JOBIA: The egg's untouched.

BLOODY FIVE: Untouched?

SOLDIER: Completely.

SECOND SOLDIER: It even got twice as big.

BLOODY FIVE: That's strange. I thought I could hit it. Couldn't someone put a few lights out now? I wish I knew who that is—dead drunk on the floor!

BEGBICK: You can have the lights out now, my Fairbaby!

SOLDIER: I for one never heard such bragging.

SECOND SOLDIER: It's a fiasco.

BLOODY FIVE: Yes, yes, you're a lot of pigs.

SOLDIERS: Bravo, bravo!

BLOODY FIVE: Urine tanks! (*He laughs. They all laugh.*) Are you putting the lights out now? Who *is* that drunk? Or is it a corpse?

URIAH: Three cheers for good old Bloody! Give him a glass of whisky.

*They roar the cheers and he drinks.*

How did you get the name Bloody Five, actually?

SOLDIERS: Show us!

BLOODY FIVE (*to* JOBIA): Shall I tell the story, ladies?

JOBIA: Oh, Bloody!

BLOODY FIVE: Then will you put the lights out if I do?

JOBIA: Tell the story, Bloody, for my sake, and I'll put the lights out!

BLOODY FIVE: This is the Lake Chad River. You are five Hindus. Their hands are tied behind their backs. I arrive with a plain ordinary army pistol. I wave it about a bit for them to see. Then I say: this pistol has misfired a number of times, it's got to be tried out. Like so. And I shoot—fall down, you there, bang! — then four times more. That was all gentlemen.

*General applause.*

Lights out!

SOLDIER: What a great soldier you are, Bloody!

SECOND SOLDIER: You give off sparks!

THIRD SOLDIER: Thrilling!

FOURTH SOLDIER: The strength of those loins must be something!

FIFTH SOLDIER: And at the same time, he's such a nice man!

SIXTH SOLDIER: So good-natured—at bottom!

URIAH: Sing us a little song, Bloody. A war song.

BLOODY FIVE: Sing—now?!

URIAH: There's nothing like music for winning a woman.

BLOODY FIVE: Is that right, Jobia?

JOBIA: Oh, Bloody!!!

BLOODY FIVE: Well, if that's what it takes to get these lights out, I'll sing a patriotic ballad I learned in school. It's called "Little Bill."

### Little Bill

I 'ave spent a lot o' time
Out in Indonesia's clime
A-watchin' 'eroes act as 'eroes will
But of all the 'ero crew
The biggest 'ero wot I knew
Wuz a sergeant o' the line called Little Bill.
For though they talk o' quiet
An' a vegetable diet
An' a nice and cozy place to rear a daughter
When it comes to real pleasure
An' the proper use o' leisure
There's nothin' like a bit o' bloody slaughter.
     Oh, it's Bill, Bill, Bill,
     An' it's kill, kill, kill,
     Just to watch the feller at it wuz a thrill!
     'E would take them Orientals

178

An' e'd melt 'em down for lentils
Would that son of a bleedin' 'ero, Little Bill.

When the sweatin' troop-train lay
In a sidin' all the day
An' the 'eat would make your bloomin' eyebrows
crawl
Bill would sit and take the sun
While 'e oiled 'is tommy-gun
An' you'd think 'e meant no bloomin' 'arm at all.
But then you'd see 'is eyes
An' you'd note to your surprise
It wuzn't just 'is body wot was 'ot.
As the tropic sun grew dimmer
Billy's 'eart came to a simmer
An' 'e'd go to it like an 'Ottentot.

Oh, it's Bill, Bill, Bill,
An' it's kill, kill, kill,
Just to see 'im boilin' over wuz a thrill!
I leave it to you to figger
Wot 'e would do to a nigger,
That son of a bleedin' 'ero, Little Bill!

Shall I e'er fergit the battle
When we 'eard ol' Bill's death rattle?
'E wuz wounded. Oh, the blood it flowed like mad.
'E wuz chokin' 'ard wiv thirst
An' the man wot spied 'im first
Wuz the one an' only friend 'e ever 'ad.
An' that friend picked up 'is 'ead
An' 'e plugged up where he bled
An' 'e give 'im rum to drink before 'is end.
An' 'e carried 'im away
An' 'e laid 'im on some 'ay.
" 'Ave ye any last request?" says this 'ere friend.
Bill's brave eyes were full o' fun
When he said: "I'll oil me gun
Just once more for soon I shall be dead."
When he took the gun in 'and
'E let fly to beat the band

179

Till 'is good and faithful friend was full o' lead.
For with Bill, Bill, Bill,
It was kill, kill, kill,
Aye, even when the foeman was a friend.
For from Genghis Khan to Nero
When you're born a bleedin' 'ero
You remain a bleedin' 'ero to the end.

SOLDIER (*enters*): Is Sergeant Charles Fairchild here? Get your company lined up in the freight station! General's orders!

BLOODY FIVE: Don't say it's me.

SECOND SOLDIER: There's no sergeant here of that name.

POLLY: Lanterns out! Jip's waking up!

BEGBICK: To hell with the lanterns! Girls, get out of here fast!

BLOODY FIVE: How about a little two-step? (*He sings and dances.*) *Two dark eyes, a purple mouth . . .*

BEGBICK: Finish packing up my canteen. I'll take care of Bloody. (*to* JOBIA:) Get the wagon ready and get gone.

BLOODY FIVE: Jobia! Jobia! Where is little Jobia! I've got to have her—or I'll be raping this drunken corpse!

BEGBICK: Come, my lad, I'll take care of you. The wagons are under way.

BLOODY FIVE: Good. In there. A woman's a woman.

BEGBICK (*exiting*): Get the tables and chairs out of here, leave the urinal to the last, and if you're not finished with this little job by the time the train whistle blows, you can have yourselves buried alive.

### Sixth Number

URIAH (*whistles*): Now comes the last Number. Funeral procession and graveside oration of Galy Gay, the last individual. Get the piano crate and put a nice funeral procession together!

180

SOLDIERS (*all carry the crate on their shoulders and sing to the tune of Chopin's Funeral March*): "Now he will drink his Irish whisky no more."

GALY GAY (*wakes up*): Who is that they're carrying?

JESSE: One who, at his final hour, was shot.

GALY GAY: What was his name?

JESSE: If I'm not mistaken, his name was Galy Gay.

GALY GAY: And what's happening to him?

JESSE: To who?

GALY GAY: To this Galy Gay.

JESSE: Oh, now he's being buried.

POLLY: Isn't that Jip? Jip, you must get up and speak at the burial of Galy Gay. For you knew him—better than we did, maybe.

GALY GAY: Yes.

JESSE: Then pace the ground between the rubber trees, and prepare the Galy Gay funeral oration!

GALY GAY *walks among the rubber trees. Next to him, never leaving his side,* JESSE *and* POLLY.

POLLY: Remember losing your tobacco pouch at Hyderabad? You said: "One time is no time."

JESSE: And the episode with the tip?

POLLY: The time you stole the lady's fish and tricked her into thinking you were her husband?

GALY GAY (*shakes his head*): The day I came out, my mother marked it in her calendar. This bundle of flesh, hair, and nails, was Me. Me.

JESSE: Yes, Jeraiah Jip. Jeraiah Jip of Tipperary.

GALY GAY: One who had to catch a nap on a wooden chair for lack of time, for, in the hut ne lived in, the fish water was on the boil. What was his name?

URIAH: Jip. Jeraiah Jip.

GALY GAY: Carry your baggage, sir?

BEGBICK (*coming out*): You know where it all leads? To death. This army is marching toward the fire-spewing guns of Tibet! Sixty thousand men and all in the same direction. This direction is from Kilkoa to Tibet, not the other way round. Now when a man finds himself in a situation like that, he has the consolation of comrades beside him, one on the left and one on the right, not to mention the dogtag round his neck with a lovely number on it so they'll know who it was when they find the body and he'll have his very own place in the grave of the many!

BLOODY FIVE (*beckoning*): Begbick! Again!

*Exit* BEGBICK. *The train whistle is heard.*

SOLDIER: The whistle!

SECOND SOLDIER: Now each man for himself!

THIRD SOLDIER: We must get our knapsacks!

*They run off.*

GALY GAY: Is that the crate he's lying inside of?

URIAH: Yes.

POLLY (*to* JESSE): If he opens it up, we're done for.

URIAH: Listen, Polly, and you, Jesse. Now that the hair by which we three hang over the abyss is breaking, listen to what I have to tell you before the last wall of Kilkoa toward eleven at night. The man we need must have a short time for reflection because he's changing for such a long time. So I draw my army pistol and threaten you both with instant death if you so much as move.

JESSE: But if he looks in the crate, the jig is up.

*They sit and wait.*

GALY GAY (*speaking*): If I looked, I'd fall dead. A face emptied out into a crate. Face of a man I used to know. Someone looked in the water, and saw that face in the shimmering surface of the water, and did drop dead; I can vouch for that. So how could I open this crate? I'm afraid. And who am I? I am a Both: there are two of me.

## The Song of the Both

Tied to a woman by a naval-cord at birth
I am a product of the ever-changing earth.
Formed like a bat, at night I seem to be
Hovering between straw hut and rubber tree.
  Who am I? Something and nothing.
  Nothing till someone calls me something.
  Should I go down into the sewer?
  Look into mystery, explore manure?
  Yes is yes, no is no, you agree?
  If I'm a man then how can there be two of me?

But I've lived in the jungle and the lowlands beneath
Where tigers question jaguars about their teeth.
Where yes and no are just the same. And so:
Do I see an elephant? Yes. That is: No.
  What's a man? Something and nothing.
  Nothing till someone calls him something.
  Nothing but what he's named by his mother.
  Nothing but what he's thought by his brother.
  Yes is no. No is yes. No? Yes!
  Why be a man when you can be a success?

(*Speaking*:) So we, the both of me, we inspect the
rain that wets us and the wind that dries us and we
build our strength by eating. (*To the three*:) You
there, can you see me at all? Where am I?

POLLY *points at him.*

Correct. What am I doing now?

POLLY: Bending your arm.

GALY GAY: Right. So I bend my arm. Am I doing it again
  now?

POLLY: Yes. A second time.

GALY GAY: I have bent my arm twice. And now?

POLLY: Now you're walking like a soldier.

GALY GAY: You walk like that?

POLLY: Just like that.

GALY GAY: What do you say, when you want something
  from me?

POLLY: Jip.

GALY GAY: Then say: walk around, Jip.

POLLY: Walk around, Jip.

SOLDIERS *enter with knapsacks.*

SOLDIERS: All aboard!

URIAH: Your funeral oration, Friend Jip, your funeral oration.

GALY GAY: Then lift Widow Begbick's piano crate with the mysterious body inside, lift it two feet in the air, then lower it six feet in Kilkoa's earth, and hear his burial oration, presented by Jeraiah Jip of Tipperary, which is no easy thing to do, as I am not prepared. But anyway, here lies Galy Gay, a man who was shot. He went off in the morning to buy a little fish, by evening had an elephant, and that same night was shot. Do not believe, my friends, that he was less than the best of men during his time on earth. He even had a straw hut on the edge of town and other things besides, about which it might be best to be silent. It was a great crime that he committed, this very good man. Well, people can say what they want, but actually it was only an oversight, and I was far too drunk, gentlemen, but a man's just a man, so he had to be shot. And now the wind is considerably cooler, as always toward morning, and we'll be going on a long journey and it may not be any too comfortable.

SOLDIERS *bang rifles.*

Why have you all packed up?

POLLY: Why, we've got to leave tonight for Tibet.

GALY GAY: Well, why haven't I packed?

POLLY: Here, cap'n. Here are your things, cap'n.

GALY GAY: What? Am I to tie that dirty old bag on my neck? It's an outrage.

SOLDIERS (*laugh*): You can't give him that knapsack.

The cap'n is a man who knows what kind of knapsack is his due.

GALY GAY: What's that? Give me that junk. I need two knapsacks anyway. This is really the end. I'll show you what Jeraiah Jip of Tipperary is made of!

POLLY: Here's my best repeating rifle for the cap'n.

JESSE: Here's my knapsack.

POLLY: Three cheers for our cap'n.

ALL: Hip hip hooray, hip hip hooray, hip hip hooray!

BEGBICK: And don't forget my billiard table, my lads!

GALY GAY: Well then! Each man help Widow Begbick so we can get moving.

SOLDIERS *carry a large package into the wagons.*

BEGBICK: That was the Human Typhoon. (*She sings:*)

### A Man's A Man 5

So, Dan, are you off on your travels tonight?
For, Dan, I am off on my travels tonight!
When you depart, such is my pride,
I must be marching at your side!
But, Dan, do you know where you're traveling to?
For I do not know where we're traveling to!
 That's all right, Dan.
 For a man is a man.
 You needn't shout.
 Really, Dan, my dear man,
 What is there to shout about?
 For men are men.
 Let us say that again:
 A man's a man.
 So it's all right, Dan.
 Kilkoa's sun shines down upon
 Six thousand soldiers and their doom.
 (When they are dead no tears are shed.
 None on the list is ever missed.)
 And so we sing: who cares on whom
 The ruddy sun of old Kilkoa shone?

185

# 10

## ON THE MOVING TRAIN: TOWARD MORNING

*Projection:* AND NOW, ON A TROOP TRAIN, ROARING TO-
WARD THE FOOTHILLS OF FAR TIBET, YOU WILL SEE THAT
MOST PHENOMENAL OF ALL PHENOMENA: REVERSE META-
MORPHOSIS: A CIVILIAN TURNS BACK INTO A SOLDIER.

GALY GAY, *the three,* BEGBICK, SOLDIERS.

JESSE: The world is frightful. You can't rely on people.

POLLY: The meanest creature alive, and the weakest, is
man. We have tramped the goddamned roads of this
all-too-endless El Dorado in dust and rain but from
the Hindu Kush to the Punjab by sun or moon, all
we have seen is treachery. This man whom we picked
up, and who now has snatched the blankets from
our beds so that we lie awake nights, is like an oil
can with a hole in it, yes and no are the same to
him, he says this today and that tomorrow.

JESSE: Polly, we have exhausted all our wisdom. Let us
go to Leocadia Begbick—she's keeping watch over
the sergeant, to see he doesn't fall off—and let's ask
her to lie down with this man so he'll feel good and
not ask questions. For though she's old, she still has
warm blood, and a man feels fine when he's in bed
with a woman. Stand up, Polly! (*They go to the*
WIDOW BEGBICK.) Widow Begbick, there's this man
who is sick. Lie down with him, will you, and act
like you'd slept with him, make him feel good.

BEGBICK (*enters, sleepy*): It'll cost you seven weeks' pay,
all of you.

URIAH: It's a deal.

BEGBICK *lies down next to* GALY GAY.

JESSE: She'll be Mrs. Jip. What more can he ask?

JESSE *covers the couple with newspapers.*

186

GALY GAY (*wakes up*): What's that shaking?

URIAH (*to the others*): It's the elephant, nibbling at your hut, you grumbler.

GALY GAY: What's that hissing?

URIAH (*to the others*): It's the fish, boiling in the water, you nice man.

GALY GAY *stands wearily up and looks through the window.*

JESSE: Act asleep.

*The three do so.*

GALY GAY: Blankets. Telegraph poles. It's a train. (*Approaching a sleeping bag.*) Hey you!

SOLDIER: Whatja want?

GALY GAY: Where are you people heading for?

SOLDIER (*opening one eye*): The front. (*He goes on sleeping.*)

GALY GAY: Soldiers. I'll lie down again and sleep till the train stops. (*Sees* BEGBICK.) A woman! Who could *she* be?

JESSE: Comrade! Good morning!

GALY GAY: Glad to see you, Mister Jesse.

JESSE: Quite a man of the world, I see! Taking your ease with a woman in full view of everyone!

GALY GAY: Yes, isn't it remarkable? Almost improper, eh? But a man isn't his own master. I wake up and, look, a woman!

JESSE: Yes, look! A woman!

GALY GAY: I often don't even know the woman I find there in the morning. To come right out with it, I don't know *her*. And, Mister Jesse, between us men, could you tell me who she is?

JESSE: Oh, you show-off! This time it's Widow Begbick —obviously. You'd know who your friend was all right, if you dipped your head in cold water. Then again, do you even know your own name?

GALY GAY: Oh yes.

JESSE: What is it?

187

GALY GAY *is silent.*

You do know your name?

GALY GAY: Yes.

JESSE: That's good. A man must know who he is when he goes to war.

GALY GAY: There's a war on?

JESSE: The Tibetan War.

GALY GAY: The Tibetan War. But if a fellow didn't know who he was, it'd be rather funny, going to war!

JESSE: Identity cards are such a good thing. The best of us has an imperfect memory. That's why we soldiers have a wallet hanging by a string around our necks, and, in this wallet, an identity card!

GALY GAY (*goes to the back, looks gloomily into his papers, and goes into his corner*): I won't think about it. I'll sit on my behind and count telegraph poles.

VOICE OF BLOODY FIVE: Where is my name that was a byword from Calcutta to Cooch Behar? I'll fix things so this train can be thrown on a junk heap like a bit of twisted stovepipe. I'll crush them like vermin, those who've done this to me! It is not important that I eat: it is important that my name's Bloody Five. It's as simple as that.

JESSE: Bloody! Wake up, Widow Begbick!

BLOODY FIVE *enters in messed-up civvies.*

GALY GAY: Has something happened to your name, maybe?

BLOODY FIVE: And I'll crush you first. Tomorrow you'll all be tin cans! (*He sees* BEGBICK *take a seat. She smiles.*) There you sit, Gomorrah! I'm Bloody Five no more—what did you do to me? Go away.

BEGBICK *laughs.*

What clothes are these? Are they suitable? What kind of head is this on my shoulders? Is it nice? Am I to sleep with you once again, Sodom?

BEGBICK: If you'd like to.

BLOODY FIVE: I would NOT like to! Go away! The eyes of the nation are upon Bloody Five. A name found three times over on every page of history!

BEGBICK: Then don't, if you wouldn't like to.

BLOODY FIVE: Don't you know what happens to my manhood when you sit there like that?

BEGBICK: "If thy manhood offend thee, pluck it out!"

BLOODY FIVE: I don't need telling twice! (*Exit.*)

GALY GAY (*calling after him*): Stop! Don't take action because of a name! A name is an uncertain thing, you can't count on it!

VOICE OF BLOODY FIVE: Here's a rope. Here's an army pistol. What do you know? Rebels are always shot. It's as simple as that! "Pack your kit bag, Johnny!" No girl will ever cost me a penny again. It's as simple as that. I needn't even take my pipe out of my mouth. I hereby assume my responsibilities. I must —to remain Bloody Five. Fire!

GALY GAY (*who has been standing at the door for some time, laughs*): Fire!

SOLDIERS *in coaches behind and front.*

Did you hear that scream?

SOLDIER: Who screamed? Someone must have got hit!

GALY GAY: I know who screamed and I know why. On account of his name, this gentleman did something very bloody to himself. He shot his sex away. I was lucky to see it, for now I know what a bloody thing it is for a man to be dissatisfied and make a fuss about a name! (*He runs to* BEGBICK.) Don't think I don't know you. I know you well: not that it matters. But tell me, how far are we from the city where we met?

BEGBICK: Many days' march. Farther every minute.

GALY GAY: How many days?

BEGBICK: Must be a hundred days' march.

GALY GAY: And how many men are there in this train for Tibet?

BEGBICK: A hundred thousand.

GALY GAY: Yes! A hundred thousand! And what do they eat?

BEGBICK: Rice and dried fish.

GALY GAY: They all eat the same?

BEGBICK: All eat the same.

GALY GAY: Yes. All eat the same.

BEGBICK: They all have blankets to sleep in, each man his own. And cotton uniforms in summer.

GALY GAY: How about the winter?

BEGBICK: Khaki uniforms.

GALY GAY: Women?

JESSE: The same.

GALY GAY: Winter and summer?

JESSE: The same women.

BEGBICK: And now you do know who you are?

GALY GAY: Jeraiah Jip is my name. (*He runs over to the three and shows his name in his papers.*)

JESSE (*and the others smile*): Correct. You know when to bring your name in, friend Jip.

GALY GAY: How about dinner?

POLLY *brings him a plate of rice.*

Yes, it is very important that I eat. (*He eats.*) How many marching days does the train cover every minute?

BEGBICK: Ten.

POLLY: So now he curls up in his seat and happily counts telegraph poles!

JESSE: A couple of guns are held under his nose and the squirrel turns into a louse—disgusting, I call it!

URIAH: Not at all. It's a proof of vitality. And as long as the real Jip doesn't turn up in the rear singing "A Man's A Man," I think our troubles are over.

SOLDIER: What's that noise?

URIAH: The thunder of cannon. We are approaching the foothills of Tibet.

GALY GAY: No more rice for me?

# 10A

## ON THE TIBETAN FRONTIER

*Projection:* IN ANTICIPATION OF A HAPPY FAMILY REUNION
THE DRUNKEN JERAIAH JIP DOUBTS WHETHER ONE MAN
IS AS GOOD AS ANOTHER.

JIP (*singing his own drunken version of "A Man's A Man"*):

Old Jip won't betray us, they all will say
For old Jip doesn't know that word, "betray."
Of all the dirty words there are
"Betray" is dirtiest by far.
And because I've been loyal to my comrades three
When I find them again, they will welcome me.
    A loyal man
    Is all right, Dan!
    Well may you shout!
    Really, Dan, my dear man,
    We've a lot to shout about.
    Men aren't just men.
    Let me say it again:
    A loyal man
    Is all right, Dan.
    Kilkoa's sun shines down upon
    Six thousand soldiers and their doom.
    But when they're dead some tears are shed.
    Some on the list are sorely missed
    The four of us do care on whom
    The ruddy sun of old Kilkoa shone.

# 11

## ON THE TIBETAN FRONTIER

*Projection:* SEE THE DESTRUCTION OF AN ENTIRE CITY.
*Second Projection:* FINAL METAMORPHOSES: JERAIAH JIP
TURNS INTO GALY GAY AND GALY GAY BECOMES A
HUMAN FIGHTING MACHINE.

JIP, *alone.*

VOICE: Thus far and no farther can His Majesty's Army
advance, for here stands the Sir el Jowr Fortress
which commands the narrow pass into Tibet.

VOICE OF GALY GAY (*behind the hill*): Run! Run! Or
we'll be too late! (*He bobs up with a cannon minus
its barrel on his back.*) Out of the train, and into
the battle! I like this! A cannon is something for a
man to live up to!

JIP: Have you seen a machine-gun unit with only three
men in it?

GALY GAY (*irresistible as a war elephant*): There's no
such thing, soldier. A unit consists of four men; one
right, one left, one behind, and one in front.

BEGBICK (*bobs up; she carries a cannon barrel on her
back*): Jippy! Don't run so fast, Jippy! You lion-
heart! You war elephant, you!

*The three turn up. Groaning, they drag their machine
gun.*

JIP: Hello, Uriah. Hello, Jesse. Hello, Polly. I'm back.

*The three pretend not to see him.*

JESSE: We must fix up the machine gun.

URIAH: The noise of the cannon is so loud, you can't hear
yourself speak.

POLLY: We must keep an eagle eye on the Sir el Jowr
Fortress.

GALY GAY: I'll shoot first. One of you carries the cannon, one throws it down to the ground, one aims it at the enemy, everybody gets cracking, and everything's all right.

BLOODY FIVE (*enters*): "Pack your kit bag, Johnny!" Well, there's that scum of a Galy Gay. Come here! What kind of a man *are* you?

GALY GAY (*smiles in his face*): No man is no man. But I won't tell anyone.

BLOODY FIVE: He's the saddest sack of the lot. I'll annihilate all four of them. It's as simple as that. But first I must get this battle going. When I've taken the Sir el Jowr Fortress, when I've heard the name Bloody Five shouted from a thousand throats, I'll have the strength to confront this chap and ask him who he is. (*Exit.*)

JIP: Hello, Jesse. Hello, Uriah. Hello, Polly. Couldn't get away any quicker. Happy to be with you again. Better late than never.

*Silence.*

POLLY: What can we do for you, sir? (*Places a plate of rice on the machine for* GALY GAY.) Wouldn't you like your rice ration, the battle is about to begin?

GALY GAY: Give it here. (*He eats.*) So, first I eat my rice ration, then I get my whisky ration, and while I eat and drink, I observe this mountain fortress, to the end of finding its weak spot. After that, it's a snap.

JIP: Your voice is different, Polly, but your sense of humor is the same. I was busy with a rather successful project of my own. Then I had to drop it. For your sake, naturally. You're not angry with me?

URIAH: You have evidently come to the wrong door, sir.

POLLY: We don't know you, sir.

JESSE: It's always possible we've met. But there's a lot of human material in the army, sir.

GALY GAY: Another rice ration! You haven't given me yours yet, Uriah.

JIP: You're all different, you know that?
URIAH: Such is life in the army.
JIP: I'm your old comrade Jip!

*The three laugh. Then* GALY GAY *starts laughing and they stop.*

GALY GAY: Another rice ration! There's a battle today, I have an appetite.

POLLY *gives him his third plate.*

JIP: Who's this who eats your rations for you?
URIAH: That is no one's business but our own.
JESSE: Look, you can never be good old Jip. Good old Jip would never have betrayed and abandoned us. Good old Jip wouldn't have got held up. And so you cannot be good old Jip.
JIP: But I am good old Jip.
URIAH: Prove it.
JIP: You are hard. It takes no prophet to know you'll come to a bad end. Give me my papers.
GALY GAY (*going over to* JIP, *plate in hand*): You're making some mistake. (*To himself:*) He's a bit cracked. (*To* JIP:) Maybe you haven't eaten for days? Like a glass of water? (*Back:*) We mustn't irritate him. You don't know where you belong? That doesn't matter. Just sit down over here till we've won the battle. And don't get too near the noise of the cannon, or you'll need great strength of soul. (*To the three:*) He doesn't know his way around. (*To* JIP:) It's true you need papers. Who'll let you run around without? Polly, run to the box on the cannon, the one with the little megaphone in it, and get the papers of that fellow you used to tease me about: Galy Gay.

POLLY *runs.*

A man who's lived in the lowlands where tigers question jaguars about their teeth knows the importance of having something on him in black and white. For nowadays everyone wants to rob you of your name. But I know what a name is good for. Why did you call me Galy Gay that time and not Mister Nobody? Dangerous games! They might have had consequences. Here! (*He gives* JIP *the identity card.*) Anything else I can do for you?

JIP: You're the best of the bunch, you have a heart. As for you others, I curse you.

GALY GAY: So you men needn't hear too much of this curse I'll make a noise with the cannon. How does it work, Widow Begbick? Show me.

JIP: May the icy wind of Tibet suck the marrow from your bones! Never shall you hear the bell in the harbor of Kilkoa, you devils. You shall march to the end of the world, and then back again, several times over! Your teacher the devil won't want you around when you're old, so you'll have to go on marching—across the Gobi Desert by day, and by night across the green waving rye fields of Wales. For you betrayed a comrade in his need. (*Exit.*)

*The three are silent.*

GALY GAY: You see, Widow Begbick, even if the fortress is made of solid bronze, if its time is come, someone need only pass by and spit on it, and it will disappear. Well, now I know both the fortress and the cannon, I shall make it in five shots.

*First shot.*

BEGBICK (*smoking a cigar*): You belong to that breed of great soldiers who in former times made the army a terror to the world. Five such fellows would be a threat even to a woman.

*Second shot.*

In the battle of the Lake Chad River it wasn't the worst men in the regiment who thought of my kisses. A night with Widow Begbick was something men

195

would give up their whisky for, something they'd save two weeks' pay for. Some of them were known all the way from Calcutta to Cooch Behar.

*Third shot.*

A single embrace of their beloved Irish colleen would calm their manly blood. You can read in the Times how tranquilly they entered the fight at Bourabay, Kamakura, and Daguth.

*Fourth shot.*

GALY GAY: What once was mountain fortress will now fall down!

*The Sir el Jowr mountain fortress starts to fall.*

*Enter* BLOODY FIVE.

BLOODY FIVE: What in God's name are you doing? If I don't stick you in this ant heap up to your neck, you'll be shooting the whole mountain range into the sea. (*He takes aim with a pistol at* GALY GAY.) Look your last upon the world! (*To the audience*:) My hand is steady as a rock.

GALY GAY: Just a moment. One more shot. Number five.

*The fifth shot is fired. A triumphant voice shouts: "The Sir el Jowr mountain fortress, which blocked the pass to Tibet, has now fallen! The Army marches into Tibet!"*

BLOODY FIVE: Just what I like to hear! An army on the march! Now! Now I confront this man. Man! Who are you?

*Voices echo in the mountain valleys: "Who are you? Who are you? Who are you?"*

GALY GAY: Just a moment.

VOICES: Who is this man who singlehanded has taken the Sir el Jowr mountain fortress?

196

GALY GAY: Polly, give me my little megaphone, will you? (*Calls through the megaphone*:) I am the man who singlehanded has taken the Sir el Jowr mountain fortress. Me! One of you! And my name—my name—is Jeraiah Jip.

VOICES: How did you do it? How did you do it?

GALY GAY (*through megaphone*): My mother used to say: Only believe. And I do. I believe one man's as good as another.

VOICES: That belief has made you the greatest soldier in His Majesty's Army. Three cheers for Jeraiah Jip, the Human Fighting Machine!

BLOODY FIVE *faints and is carried out.*

GALY GAY (*putting down the megaphone*): Forward! Your papers! We are crossing the ice-bound frontier of ancient Tibet.

*They surrender their papers.*

POLLY: Polly Baker.

JESSE: Jesse Mahoney.

URIAH: Uriah Shelley.

GALY GAY: Jeraiah Jip.

# EPILOGUE

*Re-enter* MASTER OF CEREMONIES.

MASTER: This evening's entertainment was brought to you by His Majesty's Imperial Indian Army. You have seen the metamorphosis of Galy Gay. You have seen, let's face it, a weak, homey, ineffectual fellow transformed, nay transfigured, at last into a citizen, a patriot, a soldier, and a builder of empire. It could be you. It must be you. Come forward and bear witness, yes, up here on this stage, sign your name— or, taking a little tip from the play, *sign someone else's name*—but join up, join up, join the army and see the world, your king and country need you, every nice girl loves a soldier, while Galy Gay—I mean of course Jeraiah Jip—while Jeraiah Jip sings the refrain of our Recruiting Song. The verse, you remember, is sung by Private Johnny Jones. Johnny!

## *Recruiting Song*

JOHNNY JONES:

There was a time when priest and pedagogue
                         besought me
To think that I was I and you were you.
The very songs my dear old mother taught me
Said: Be yourself! And: To thyself be true.
But later on a million brothers told me:
You are not you, I am by no means I.
And this the gospel that my brothers sold me:
Be someone else! Be Tommy! Go on: try!

GALY GAY:

Join the army, Tommy,
We're off to Calcutta tonight!
Snow is not snow, Tommy,
And black is white.
Pack your kit bag, Tommy,
And fight, fight, fight,
For right is wrong, Tommy,
And might is right.

198

# The Elephant Calf

# ADAPTOR'S NOTE

The text that follows is not an adaptation but is as close as I could make it to the German original.

When the play was produced, it was adapted to the following extent. First, a prologue was supplied.

For Mister Brecht there's nothing easier than
To prove conclusively a man's a man.
But this you know. Tonight our poet sings
That he can prove a lot of other things.
That men are elephants. That men are trees.
That men are crescent moons. Did someone sneeze?
This, then, tonight is Mister Brecht's contention:

HE CAN PROVE ANY GODDAMNED THING YOU
    LIKE TO MENTION.

Next, since no Brecht lyric beginning "Wipe your jack-boots, Johnny" is extant, another cue was substituted to lead into the singing of "Orge's Hymn" (taken from *Baal,* above). Third, a cue was written in to provide the occasion to sing "The Benares Song" at the very end. This song was written in English by Bertolt Brecht and first published in his book of poems, *Die Hauspostille* (1927). The tune Brecht provided for "Orge's Hymn" is given on p. 96 above. Words and tune of "The Benares Song" are as follows:

Benares Song

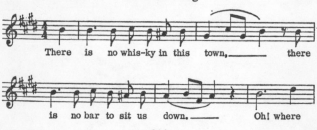

is the te-le-phone? Is here no te-le-phone? Oh!
Sir, God damn me: No! Let's — go to Be-
na-res, where — the sun is shin-ing,
let's — go to Be-na-res! John-ny let us go.

2

There is no money in this land
There is no girl with whom to shake hands
Oh!
Where is the telephone?
Is here no telephone?
Oh Sir, God damn me:
No!
    Let's go to Benares
    Where the sun is shining
    Let's go to Benares!
    Johnny, let us go.

3

There is not much fun on this star
There is no door that is ajar
Oh!
Where is the telephone?
Is here no telephone?

201

Oh, Sir, God damn me:
No!

> Worst of all, Benares
> Is said to have perished in an earthquake!
> Oh! our good Benares!
> Oh, where shall we go!
> Worst of all, Benares
> Is said to have perished in an earthquake!
> Oh! our good Benares!
> Oh, where shall we go!

Accompaniments were composed for these two tunes by Eric Regener, who also composed the music for the "Uganda Song" ("Oh dear, what fun we had in old Uganda!"); he did not make a song of the Monologue of a Mother's Grief but made of it a "Melodram" (rhetorical speaking against a musical background).

*Das Elefantenkalb oder die Beweisbarkeit Jeglicher Behauptung* was published as an appendix to *A Man's A Man* in the 1927 edition (Im Propyläen-Verlag, Berlin, copyright 1926 by Arcadia Verlag, Berlin). Its relation to *A Man's A Man* is none too clear, as Galy Gay, though he has replaced Jeraiah, is by no means the mechanical monster of the final scene of the longer play. Brecht planned *A Man's A Man* several times, and one of his conceptions seems to have been of a Galy Gay who turned simply into a soldier, not a superman: in any event, this is the formula of *The Elephant Calf*.

It would surely be difficult to put this one-act across as the interlude ("Zwischenspiel") to be played in the lobby, which Brecht later declared it to be. How could the audience understand it if it were inserted *before* the scenes in which Galy Gay turns into a soldier? It can be played as an epilogue if allowances are made for the differences in conception just mentioned. But it is really *A Man's A Man* all over again, though in a slightly different interpretation of the fable, and only fully intelligible to an audience that already knows the fable. It is not "absurd." Zany in style, it tells a story that is no more zany than it is true: again an innocent Galy Gay is victimized, again his trial is an outrageous frame-up and reason is enlisted in the cause of cruelty and *un*reason, again Galy Gay puts up opposition only just so long. The little play culminates in the apparently sudden turnabout when he says: "By the way, I wouldn't like you to think *I* don't accept what you have just seen."

It is the business of the performers of *The Elephant Calf* to make this passive acceptance of things as horrifying as the active acceptance of them in *A Man's A Man*. The cool, trivial, indifference of this Galy Gay is even less human than the fascistic frenzy of the other one.

—E.B.

February, 1963

# THE ELEPHANT CALF

or

The provability of any and every contention

by

BERTOLT BRECHT

*English version by*
ERIC BENTLEY

# CAST

First produced by the Theatre for Ideas, 112 West 21st Street, New York City, January 6th, 1963, directed by Maurice Edwards, music by Eric Regener, with the following cast:

| | |
|---|---|
| POLLY BAKER | Clifton James |
| URIAH SHELLEY | Eric Berger |
| JESSE MAHONEY | David Spielberg |
| GALY GAY (JERAIAH JIP) | John Heffernan |

SOLDIERS: John Abbey, Ralf von Boda, Louis Gordon, John Grant, Duncan Hoxworth, Eric Regener (Pianist).

*Theatre: a platform beneath a few rubber trees. Chairs in front of it. This "theatre" is seen from the side: we see both behind and in front of the curtain.*

POLLY (*in front of the curtain*): So that dramatic art can have its full effect on you, you are requested to smoke to your heart's content. Our artists are the best in the world, the drinks are one hundred percent, the chairs are comfortable, bets will be taken at the bar on how the plot comes out, and the act curtain will fall each time the audience bets. And please don't shoot the piano player, he's doing his best. Whoever can't immediately understand the plot needn't fret, it is incomprehensible. If all you want to see is something that makes sense, go to the urinal. Your money isn't returnable in any case. This

is our comrade Jip who has the honor of playing Pal
Jacky the elephant calf. If you consider it too hard
a job, my answer is: a theatrical artist must be able
to do everything.

SOLDIER (*out front*): Bravo!

POLLY: Jesse Mahoney here will play Pal Jacky's mother,
and Uriah Shelley, connoisseur of international horse
racing will play the Moon. You will also have the
pleasure of seeing me, Polly Baker, in the featured
role of the Banana Tree.

SOLDIERS: Get going. And remember: ten cents for such
junk is highway robbery.

POLLY: We are not going to let ourselves be influenced
by such vulgar aspersions. The play deals, in the
main, with a crime this elephant calf committed. I
tell you this so we needn't keep interrupting.

URIAH (*behind the curtain*): Allegedly committed.

POLLY: Quite right. That's what comes of studying only
my own role. Actually, the elephant calf is innocent.

SOLDIERS (*in rhythm*): Get going! Get going! Get going!

POLLY: One moment. (*Steps behind the curtain.*) I fear
we may have charged too much for admission, what
do you say?

URIAH: This is hardly the moment to think of such things.
This is the time to take the plunge!

POLLY: It's just that the play is so weak. You probably
don't quite recall, Jesse, what it was like when we
did it in the regular theatre. And the parts you've
forgotten, Jesse, were the main things, I believe.
Wait. Just a minute. I want to go to the bathroom.

*Curtain up.*

I am the Banana Tree.

SOLDIER: At long last!

POLLY: The Banana Tree: Judge of the Jungle. Here I
stand, on the parched plateau of the southern Pun-

jab—as I have done since the invention of elephants. Sometimes, mostly of an evening, the Moon comes up to me, bringing charges—against an elephant calf, for example.

URIAH: Not so fast. That's half the play. For ten cents! (*He—i.e., the Moon—rises.*)

POLLY: Oh, Moon, hello! Where are you coming from so late in the evening?

URIAH: I've been hearing quite a story about an elephant calf—

POLLY: You're bringing charges against it?

URIAH: Well, naturally.

POLLY: So the elephant calf's committed a crime?

URIAH: Right! You have guessed, and you have guessed right! Effective proof of your perspicuity! Nothing escapes you!

POLLY: Think nothing of it. The elephant calf has murdered its mother, hasn't it?

URIAH: It has, yes.

POLLY: And that's terrible.

URIAH: It's frightful.

POLLY: If only I hadn't mislaid my horn-rimmed glasses!

URIAH: Oh, I have a pair here, as it happens, maybe they're right for you.

POLLY: They'd certainly be right if they also had lenses in them but they have no lenses in them.

URIAH: Still they're better than nothing.

POLLY: Where's the laugh on that line?

URIAH: Yes, I wonder. So I'll bring these charges against the Moon. I mean: against the elephant calf.

PAL JACKY *comes slowly on.*

POLLY: Ah, yes, here's the nice little elephant calf. Where are you coming from, hm?

GALY GAY: I'm the elephant calf. Seven Rajahs presided at my cradle. What are you laughing at, Moon?

URIAH: Just go right on talking, Elephant.

GALY GAY: My name is Pal Jacky. I'm taking a walk.

POLLY: So you've smashed your mother to bits, have you?

GALY GAY: I smashed her milk jar to bits.

URIAH: And it cracked her skull, eh?

GALY GAY: No, Moon, it fell on a stone.

POLLY: But you did do it, as sure as I'm a Banana Tree?

URIAH: And as sure as I'm the Moon, I'll prove it. My first proof is this lady here.

*JESSE comes on as* PAL JACKY's *mother.*

POLLY: Who's this?

URIAH: The mother.

POLLY: Yes. Remarkable when you come to think of it.

URIAH: Not at all.

POLLY: I find it bizarre—that she's here, I mean.

URIAH: I don't.

POLLY: Then she can stay. Only: it must be proved. Naturally.

URIAH: Yes. You're the judge.

POLLY: Yes. Well then, Elephant Calf, prove you didn't murder your mother.

SOLDIER (*out front*): And with her standing there!

URIAH (*to him*): That's just it, though.

SOLDIER: Even the beginning is lousy. With the mother standing there! This play has no further interest for me.

JESSE: I am this elephant calf's mother. I'll take a bet my little Jacky can prove he's not a murderer. Can't you, Jacky pal?

URIAH: And I'll take a bet he can never in this world prove it.

POLLY (*roaring*): Curtain!

*The audience goes silently to the bar, then orders cocktails in loud, clamorous voices.*

POLLY (*behind the curtain*): Went pretty nicely. No cat-calls at all.

GALY GAY: But why did no one clap?

JESSE: Maybe they're enthralled.

209

POLLY: It's so interesting, you see.

URIAH: If we could only show them the thighs of a few chorus girls, they'd trample these benches under foot. Go out on stage. We must try the betting.

POLLY (*comes out*): Gentlemen—

SOLDIERS: Cut it out. The intermission's too short. First let us drink: we need to—in the circumstances.

POLLY: We just wondered if maybe you wouldn't like to take bets. I mean on each side. Mother versus Moon.

SOLDIERS: The gall of the man. So that's how they'll get more money out of us. Well, let's wait till this thing gets moving. The beginning is never any good.

POLLY: All right. Whoever wants to back the Mother, this way. (*Nobody comes forward.*) Those who're for the Moon, this way.

*Nobody comes forward.* POLLY *goes off, very upset.*

URIAH (*behind the curtain*): Did they bet?

POLLY: Not specially. They think the best is yet to come. That upsets me.

JESSE: They're drinking desperately. It's as if they couldn't bear to go on listening.

URIAH: We'll have to try music. It'll cheer them up.

POLLY (*comes on*): From now on, phonograph music!

*Curtain up.*

Step this way, Moon, Mother, and Elephant, and you shall forthwith see this enigmatic crime completely cleared up. (*To the audience*:) So will you. How do you intend to conceal the fact anyway that you, Pal Jacky, stabbed your worthy mother to death?

GALY GAY: How *can* I have done so? Being but a girl, and frail?

POLLY: Oh, I see. Well then, I contend that you, Pal Jacky, are not a girl as you claim. Just listen to my first great proof. I remember a bizarre story from my childhood in Whitechapel—

SOLDIER: The Southern Punjab!

210

*Ringing laughter.*

POLLY: —Southern Punjab. There was this man who put on a girl's skirt so he wouldn't have to go to war. The sergeant came along with a bullet which he threw in his lap and because he didn't spread his legs out, as girls do, to catch the bullet in his skirt, the sergeant knew it was a man, as in this case. (*They enact this.*) So. You have all seen that the little elephant is a man. Curtain!

*Curtain. Feeble applause.*

POLLY: We have a hit on our hands, just listen. Get that curtain up. Curtain call!

*They bow. Curtain. No applause.*

URIAH: They're loaded with hostility. We can't win.

JESSE: We'll just have to stop, and give them their money back. To be lynched or not to be lynched, that is the question, that's how horribly far things have gone. Just look out front!

URIAH: Give 'em their money back? Never! No theatre in the world can afford *that!*

SOLDIERS: Tomorrow: forward to Tibet! You know, Georgie, these may be the last rubber trees you'll ever drink four-cent cocktails under! The weather isn't pleasant enough for a war, or it'd be nice to stay right here—only it's up north that the game's to be played!

SOLDIER: Anyhow why not let loose with a little song, such as: "Wipe your jackboots, Johnny"?

SOLDIERS: Great! (*They sing:*) "Wipe your . . ."

URIAH: They're singing on their own now. We must proceed!

POLLY: I wish I was in the auditorium. That Johnny thing is a lovely song. If only *we* had thought of something like that. Let's get going.

*Curtain up.*

211

After . . . (*He combats the song.*) Now that the elephant calf—

SOLDIER: Still that elephant calf!

POLLY: I said, now that the elephant—

SOLDIER: Calf!

POLLY: Now that . . . a certain animal has been unmasked by my first great proof as a swindler, there comes my second, and still greater, proof.

SOLDIER: Can't you leave this one out, Polly?

URIAH: Yeah, Polly, just you dare.

POLLY: I'm contending that you are a murderer, Pal Jacky. So prove to me that you cannot murder—the Moon, for instance.

SOLDIER: But this is all wrong. The Banana Tree must prove that.

POLLY: Precisely. Just watch. This is a specially exciting point in the drama. "You must prove," I was saying, "that you could never murder—the Moon, for instance. So climb up this clinging creeper here and bring your knife with you."

GALY GAY *does so. The creeper is a rope-ladder which the Moon holds above him.*

SOLDIER (*getting a few who want to go on singing to be quiet*): Quiet! It's not so easy to climb up that thing, he can't see out of that elephant's head!

JESSE: This has *got* to work! Now, Uriah, a voice of thunder!

URIAH *lets out a cry.*

POLLY: What's the matter, Moon? Why the shouting?

URIAH: Because it hurts like crazy! This must definitely be a murderer who's coming up to me!

GALY GAY: Hang this rope-ladder on a bough, Uriah! I am very heavy.

URIAH: Oh! it's tearing my hand off! My hand! My hand! It's tearing my hand off!

POLLY: Just look! Look!

> GALY GAY *has* URIAH's—*artificial*—*hand in his hand; he exhibits it.*

JESSE: That's bad, Jacky. I wouldn't have thought it of you. You're not my child.

URIAH (*holding up his stump*): I testify that he is a murderer!

POLLY: Now all take a look at the bloody stump with which he testifies that you, Pal Jacky, have not proved that you cannot commit murder, for you have so dealt with the Moon that he will certainly bleed to death by morning. Curtain! (*Curtain. He steps out.*) Now if there are any bets—go to the bar!

SOLDIERS (*go to bet*): One cent on the Moon. Half a cent on the Elephant.

URIAH: They bite, you see! You'd have them eating out of your hand, Jesse, if you did your Monologue of a Mother's Grief.

*Curtain up.*

JESSE:

Of all our earthly or unearthly joys
There's nothing like a mother—is there, boys?
A mother's heart has fed you with her blood.
A mother's hand has given you your food.
A mother's eye has shielded you from wrath.
A mother's foot has kicked the stones from your
                                                   path.

*Laughter.*

When mother's body goes beneath the sod
A noble soul flies, lickety-split, to God.

*Laughter.*

Hear now a mother cry in her great woe:
"To think this beast was once my embryo!"

*Big, long laughter.*

SOLDIERS: Encore! Worth the price of admission—all ten cents of it! Great! Hurrah! Three cheers for Mother! Hip, hip, hurray!

*The curtain falls.*

URIAH: Get cracking. This is success. On stage!

*Curtain up.*

POLLY: I have proved that you are a man who can commit murder. Now I have a question for you, Jacky. Do you contend that this is your mother?

SOLDIERS: Damned unjust, this business, it goes against the grain. But it's philosophical, all right. They're bound to have some kind of happy ending ready, we can depend on that. Quiet!

POLLY: Naturally I wouldn't contend that any son of woman would touch a hair of his very own Mummy-wummy, not in territory governed by old England.

*Bravos.*

Rule Britannia!

*All sing: "Rule Britannia."*

Thank you, gentlemen. So long as that soul-shaking song issues from rough, manly throats all is well with old England. To proceed. Since, O Pal Jacky, you have murdered this universally loved lady, this truly great artist,

*Bravos.*

it obviously cannot be the case, can it, Jacky, old man, that you are the son—or daughter—of the said distinguished lady?

*Bravos.*

No. What a banana tree contends he can also prove.

*Applause.*

214

Therefore, O Moon of Cooch Behar, take a piece of billiard chalk and draw a good solid circle right on the middle of this stage. Then take a plain ordinary piece of rope in your hand and wait till this mother —stricken to the very heart, as she is—steps into the circle which you have now finished drawing, if rather badly. Place this rope—with care—about her snow-white neck.

SOLDIERS: Her lovely snow-white neck, her lovely snow-white neck!

POLLY: Quite right. But you—the alleged Pal Jacky— take the other end of this rope of justice and stand outside the circle opposite the Moon. Right. Now, woman, I put a question to you: Have you given birth to a murderer? No answer? Well then, I only wanted to show you, gentlemen, that the very Mother, whom you now see before you, turns away from her fallen child. But in a minute I'll show you even more than that. For now the fearful sun of justice will shine into the secret depths.

SOLDIERS: Now, Polly, don't go too far! Psst!

POLLY: Pal Jacky, for the last time: do you still contend that you are the son of this unhappy creature here?

GALY GAY: Yes.

POLLY: I see. I see. So you're her son, eh? Not long ago you would have it you were her daughter. But then you don't aim at one hundred percent accuracy, do you? We go on now to the principal proof, the first and last and all-embracing proof, a proof which will satisfy you all, gentlemen. If, Jacky, you are the child of this mother, then the strength will be given to you to pull her out of the circle on that side. So much is clear.

SOLDIERS: Crystal clear. Clear as *cracked* crystal. Stop. This is all wrong. Jacky: stand by the truth!

POLLY: I shall count three. One. Two. Three.

GALY GAY *pulls* JESSE *out of the circle.*

215

JESSE: Hey! Stop! God damn it! What are you up to! Ouch, my neck!

SOLDIERS: Neck, neck? Pull, Jacky! Now stop—he's as blue as shell fish!

JESSE: Help!

GALY GAY: Out of the circle! She's out of the circle!

POLLY: Well! And what do you all say to that? Have you ever seen such brutality? All I can say is: here unnatural deceit gets its deserts.

*Big applause.*

POLLY: Elephant Calf, you have grossly deceived yourself. By this brutal pulling, you have proved, not what you intended, but something else, namely, that never never never can you be the son—or daughter—of this unhappy, martyred mother. You have pulled the truth into the light, Jacky my pal!

SOLDIERS: Oho! Great! Hideous! A nice family! Be off, Jacky boy, it's all up with you. A put-up job. Just stand by the truth, Jacky.

POLLY: There, gentlemen: I think that should suffice. The first and last proof, I think you will agree, has been brought to harbor. And now, listen carefully, gentlemen, and let me ask those to listen also who at first thought it necessary to raise a rumpus here, as also those who bet their good pennies that this miserable elephant calf, punctured, as he now is, by proofs, is not a murderer, this elephant calf *is* a murderer! This elephant calf, which is not the daughter of this worthy mother as it contended, but the son, as I have proved, is also not the son, as you have seen, because it is not even the child of this matron, whom it murdered, though she stands here before your very eyes and acts like nothing had happened, which after all is natural, though on the other hand it is unprecedented, which I am also ready to prove, in fact I will prove anything you like, and will contend even more than that, and never be put off but always insist on what I see the way I see it, and prove it

216

too, for, I ask you: what is anything without proof?

*The applause ever more tumultuous.*

POLLY: Without proof a man is not even a man but an Orang-Utang, as Darwin proved, and then where is progress? And if you so much as bat an eyelash, you miserable, little nothing of a lie-dripping elephant calf—phony to the marrow, as you are—then I will prove anyhow, and I'm going to do it in any case, yes, actually this is my main point, gentlemen, that this elephant calf is not an elephant calf anyhow, but at best Jeraiah Jip of Tipperary.

*Tumultuous applause.*

SOLDIERS: Hooray!
GALY GAY: That's not right.
POLLY: Why not? Why shouldn't it be right?
GALY GAY: It's not what the play says. Take it back.
POLLY: But you *are* a murderer.
GALY GAY: That's not true.
POLLY: But I've proved it. Proved, proved, proved!

> GALY GAY, *moaning, hurls himself at the banana tree.*
> *Under this terrific assault, the tree collapses.*

POLLY (*collapsing*): You see! You see!
URIAH: So. Now you are a murderer.
POLLY (*with a groan*): And I proved it.
> *Curtain.*

URIAH: The song—quick!
THE FOUR PLAYERS (*get quickly in front of the curtain to sing*):
> Oh dear, what fun we had in old Uganda!
> A nickel for a chair on the veranda!
> Oh dear, the poker games with Mister Tiger!
> We did twice as well, I'll tell you that,
> When we bet the hide of Daddy Kruger
> And Tiger bet his bowler hat!
> Oh dear, the moon shone bright in old Uganda!

The air was cool, the trains went root-toot-toot!
Not every one has got the money
For poker with this very funny
Tiger in his business suit.
(A nickel for a chair on the veranda.)

SOLDIER: It's over? But it's so unjust! Does that make a good ending? You can't just stop there. Leave the curtain up. Go on with the play!

POLLY: What? There's no more script! Be reasonable. The play is over.

SOLDIERS: What gall! I never knew anything like it. Crap of the purest water! Against good sense! (*A bunch of them go up on stage and talk earnestly.*) We want our money back. Either the elephant calf ends up all right or you'll put our money down on your bar, every red cent of it, you Moon of Cooch Behar!

POLLY: What you saw on this stage was the naked truth, I would have you know.

SOLDIERS: In that case, you are all about to see the whites of truth's eyes!

POLLY: You only say that because you know nothing of Art. You don't know how to behave to artists.

SOLDIERS: We can do without all this talk!

GALY GAY: By the way, I wouldn't like you to think *I* don't accept what you have just seen.

POLLY: Thank you, cap'n.

GALY GAY: And to get ahead of the game a little bit, I would like to invite to a little eight-round boxing match with four-ounce gloves whichever gentleman, whichever bizarre gentleman, asks for his money back with the greatest urgency.

SOLDIERS: That would be Townley. Townley: forward! Wipe this little elephant's little snout off!

GALY GAY: Very well, so we shall now see, I believe, whether it was the truth that we staged here for you, or whether it was theatre—good or bad—my fine fellows!

*All off to the boxing match.*